The TEN COMMANDMENTS

AN EXPOSITORY SERMON SERIES

NORBERT C. OESCH

CPH
SAINT LOUIS

CONTENTS

THE FIRST COMMANDMENT

SERMON

Grace, mercy and peace, in the name of our triune God: the Father, the Son, and the Holy Spirit. Amen.

Today we start off on a spiritual journey, one that's not so new, but one that will be, I pray, renewing. We are going to explore the fundamentals for the expression of the Christian faith: the Ten Commandments.

I also am inviting you to participate in two "disciplines" as part of this journey. One is personal or family devotions. We have prepared four devotions for each week during this series. Those of you who have been having devotions daily, don't go back to just four, okay? It'll be just fine to keep up that daily exercise. For the rest who haven't started that discipline: four times a week.

In order to remind you and help you grow in a second discipline, we have put together little "table cards" that look like this. *[Display one.]* Fold them on the lines, tape the bottom together, and put them out on your table or wherever you will be doing your devotions—where the cards can be seen. Every week the theme and the commandment will be on one side. This week: "I am the LORD your God" and "You shall have no other gods before me." On the back will be a related Bible passage that I am asking you to memorize along with the commandment. Ah-ha; exercise of the mind!

Actually, the memorization will be easy. You'll see the words every day during the week. Sometimes you'll walk by, see it, and repeat it. Let's practice on the one for this week. The commandment: "You shall have no other gods before me." The passage: "Praise be to the Lord, the God of Israel, because he has come and has redeemed his people" (Luke 1:68). So simple to learn!

My brothers and sisters, if we give ourselves to this, God is going to bless our discipline, because the words we memorize and study are *his* Word. So I ask you to encourage one another in this discipline beginning this very week. Perhaps today, perhaps tomorrow, start your devotion. Put those cards up, start your memorizing, and let's give ourselves to that task.

Today we study the First Commandment. The theme is "I am the LORD *your* God."

I've accented *"your* God," because it is in those words that we find the Gospel.

The commandment, "You shall have no other gods before me," means we should fear and love and trust in God above everything else.

Recall the setting when the commandments were first given. God had appointed Moses to deliver the Israelites, and through signs and miracles and God's strong right arm that's what Moses did. He led them out of Egypt to Mount Sinai, where they gathered to worship. Then God called Moses up onto the mountain. When he was up there, God inscribed the Ten Commandments and gave them to Moses to deliver to the children of Israel. The commandments start with a prolog, a wonderful rationale: "I am the LORD your God, who brought you out of Egypt, out of the land of slavery" (Ex. 20:2). Then comes the First Commandment: "You shall have no other gods before me."

To understand the prolog, think in terms of God establishing a covenant, a legal agreement with his people. The particular form that he uses here is an ancient form: the Hittite suzerain treaty. There were many different kinds of treaties that were drawn up in the time of Moses and the early ancestors in the Scriptures, but this particular one was of the type that a suzerain, a sovereign lord, a king over considerable territory, would establish with his vassal kings. It was unilateral in the sense that the suzerain alone dictated the rules and the way the agreement would work; but it was bilateral in the sense that both parties had responsibilities. The suzerain was saying, "As long as we live in this relationship I will be your king, and I will watch over you. I will protect you from your enemies, and I will provide for you a wonderful life in my realm. But you must keep the stipulations."

All suzerain covenants started with a historical prolog that outlined what the great king had done. It then listed the stipulations of the covenant, and then the blessings and cursings—"If you keep these stipulations, these are the blessings you will receive; if you don't, here are the curses that you can expect." The treaty usually ended by listing the witnesses to the sealing of the covenant. Those witnesses could be mountains, people, or a god. Finally the treaty would be enshrined in some holy place, so the people would always be reminded that the covenant had been established.

This is the form that God used as he formulated his relationship with his people at Sinai. He says in effect, "Look what I have done for you. I did not conquer you like a human king. No; I freed you, and I'm giving you a land of your own. Nor will I ever abandon you to another god—as if there were one. These are my precious gifts to you."

That's the background. Then God continues with the first stipulation: "You shall have no other gods before me." Like a suzerain who is going to be gracious to all who live in his kingdom, he says, "I will be your king, and I demand absolute allegiance. You can have no other king, no other suzerain, no other sovereign than me."

God says the same thing to you and me: "I gave myself to you; I am your

God; by my Son's death I have made you my people. But there can be no competitors. You must have no other gods."

We can understand that kind of contract. If you are married, you have made a similar solemn agreement: "I will give myself to you, my dear spouse; but there is one thing that I demand, and that is that you give yourself exclusively to me. You cannot have another spouse—or lover. It is to be I and I alone."

The difference, of course, is that God is not a human spouse; he is God—which leads us to ask the question: What is a god?

Ultimately, a god is anything on which we rely for good things and for refuge. In Phil. 3:19, the stomach is referred to as a god. In Prov. 3:5, it's a person's own understanding. In Jesus' parable of the rich fool (Luke 12:16–20), it's riches. In Matt. 10:37, it's parents.

When we hear all that, we know we have a problem. We're supposed to have *no* other gods, but the Law reveals that we do. That's one of the purposes of the Law: to mirror to us our sin. And this First Commandment immediately leads us to confess, "Uh-oh; I have a problem because I have other gods. That's my fallen nature."

Which "other gods" do you have? Money? I believe that's the foremost idol in the Western world. Oh, is it ever an idol! Do you excuse yourself? If so, ask yourself how you would react if you were told that tomorrow morning at 9 a.m. you would lose all your income. When we're up against losing it, then we begin to see how much we have looked to a certain thing for security.

Or, what about people? Are they your "other god"? We live in relationships, and we need relationships. How often have I heard good Christian people, in the face of seeing some loved one very sick and maybe dying, say, "I don't know if I can live without this person." Can't live without them? Have they become god?

Thus it is that this First Commandment, "You shall have no other gods before me," comes as a mirror and shows our sinfulness. We have to say, "I am guilty. Lord, forgive."

Then comes the good news—and in two parts. You see it first as it comes in the words of the prolog: "I am the LORD *your* God." The good news is that God has given himself in Jesus Christ to us. In what sense and how are we going to understand that in the light of our sinfulness? We have to go back to the suzerain again.

If the people underneath the suzerain broke the covenant, then the agreement was off. The suzerain no longer had any responsibility to protect the people or provide for them. In fact, the treaties usually specified that he would come to reap vengeance upon them. They would experience his wrath, and then they would be abandoned.

The Israelites had a deliverer in Moses, who was sent by God to show them the way out of their bondage. So we too need a deliverer. Our sinfulness is like a slavery and a bondage. We need to be delivered from it in order that God's vengeance and anger and wrath will not come upon us, that we will not be abandoned forever.

God has sent his Son Jesus Christ to be our deliverer. Jesus took upon himself God's own wrath for our breaking the covenant. Jesus accepted that very abandonment that we were to experience from the Holy Suzerain. On the cross Jesus endured the vengeance of God; he endured the wrath and abandonment. Jesus himself said, "My God, my God, why have you forsaken me?" (Matt. 27:46). He suffered that vengeance, wrath, and abandonment in our place. As a result, our suzerain, our Lord God says, "Because restitution has been made, I make a new covenant with you, a covenant based upon the forgiveness of sins. I restore you to be my people. Now you are my sons and daughters; and despite your sin, I am your God. I am your benefactor, and I will provide for you; I will care for you."

God also says, "Furthermore, I am giving you the power to love me above everything else." Thus he begins to create into our lives a filial relationship, that is, one that a son or daughter might have with a loving parent. Not a relationship of fear like a servant or slave, but a relationship of love that grows out of being loved by our heavenly Father, who has shown time and again that we can trust him and cast all our cares on him because he cares for us. He never abandons us.

In his Word, God reaches out his hand and says "Trust me." Then his Holy Spirit enters our hearts, and we begin to trust him as he begins to work love for him in our hearts.

Why are you here? You could be on the beach, maybe in the mountains, maybe at home. Why are you here? Because God has worked not only trust but also love in your heart for him, and you have begun to respond to him. And having worked love and trust, he now also begins to work obedience in your lives.

Have you ever watched in real life or in a nature film the way young raccoons obey their parents? At some predetermined signal by one of the parents the young ones go right up a tree about 30 feet and stay there till the adult is finished hunting for food. The young hang on, play, perhaps sleep, whatever, for half an hour or so. They will not come down. Then all of a sudden, the parents come back and, with no visible signal, those pups come down.

Don't you wish all kids were that obedient? I'm sure God wishes the same thing about all of us. The difference is, he not only wishes it, he has done something about it. He works in our lives the power to begin to obey him.

And thus, as his people, we now hear again the commandment, "You shall have no other gods before me." And because of God's love in Christ, our hearts say "Amen."

I Am the God

Invocation: Dear Father, help us to understand that you are the Lord of our lives.

Text: I am the LORD your God … You shall have no other gods. Ex. 20:2, 3

Insight: When Moses stood at the burning bush and asked the name of who was talking to him, the response came, "I AM WHO I AM." In other words, the only true, real God.

Elijah McCoy had a boring job back at the time when steam engines pulled trains across the United States. Elijah worked on a train that stopped at every small town along the track to pick up more freight or maybe a passenger or two.

Whenever the train stopped, Elijah had to hop off to oil the steam engine. Then he'd hop back on, and the train would chug down the track once again. Off, oil, on. Off, oil, on. Off, oil, on.

Elijah soon got tired of the monotony and invented an automatic oiling system. It worked so well that before long all steam engines were equipped with his invention.

Then Elijah began inventing other things to make jobs easier. Other people tried to copy Elijah McCoy's inventions but only his worked reliably. His inventions became so famous that customers soon demanded the "real McCoy"—no substitute! Still today "the real McCoy" means the real thing, not a copy.

The one who spoke to Moses and the one who speaks to us in Scripture and the one who came in the flesh at Bethlehem is "the real McCoy." A copy just won't do.

Jesus is our God. He is the Lord of our lives. Though other things may try to be Lord of our lives, God reminds us that only he is our Lord.

Prayer: Lord of all, we ask you to forgive us when we allow other things to lead and influence us. Help us to show that you are Lord of our lives by …

I Am the LORD [Yahweh]

Invocation: Father, as we gather together as a family—your family—help us to focus upon your name that you revealed to Moses: I AM.

Text: I am the LORD your God … You shall have no other gods. Ex. 20:2, 3

Insight: Do you know the meaning of your name? For instance, *Brian* means "mighty leader"; *Sara* means "princess." Throughout the Old Testament, God called Himself *Yahweh*, which is sometimes translated as *Jehovah*, but is usually written in our Bibles as "the LORD." *Yahweh* means "He is," which may seem like a strange name—until we know what it means for us. It means that God is always with us. Therefore his name is "He Is."

Our God is the same all the time, from the very beginning. He does not change. Whenever we need him, he is there. Wherever we go, he is there. Whenever we're in trouble, he is with us. In fact, he sent his only Son, Jesus, to die for us to bail us out of our trouble of sin. He is present in forgiveness.

He is also present for us to worship and praise. In fact, he wants us to worship and praise him all the time—by ourselves, with our families, and also with fellow Christians at church.

How happy we are, because God has chosen us to be his! How glad we are that his name is *Yahweh*, "He Is," because he is *always* available for us, our families, and our church!

Prayer: Dear Lord, thank you for always being there for me. Many times I forget that you are always available for me. Help me to pray for …

I Am the Lord Your God

Invocation: Heavenly Father, help us to realize your awesomeness and to see that you are our strong rock.

Text: I am the Lord your God … You shall have no other gods. Ex. 20:2, 3

Insight: Who is God? Only one man has ever seen God: Jesus. Moses almost saw him, but only from the back. No man other than Jesus can look into God's face, because it is too bright. God is really a mystery. God cannot be understood. God cannot be seen. He is too superior (Is. 55:8–9).

Thank God, we *cannot* understand God. If we could, then he would be equal with us; and if equal with us, he could not help us. Help, you know, must come from someone stronger and higher than the one in need of help.

Aren't you glad that God is greater than you, that he knows everything, can do anything, is everywhere? Doesn't it make you full of joy to know that God is the one whom you can trust?

Picture the Rock of Gibraltar, nearly 1,400 feet high, three-fourths of a mile wide, and over two miles long. It has steep sides, and the ocean surrounds it on three sides. With its military fortifications, it is such a powerful stronghold that no one has been able to conquer it for over 200 years. It's a very safe place to hide.

You and I, though, have an even better place to go for safety from danger and for help in trouble. Like David, we can say, "[God] is my rock and my salvation" (Ps. 62:6). God has sent his own Son to take away our sins and to rescue us from the devil. Sin and Satan can no longer harm us. Why would we want any other god?

Prayer: O God, our rock, our fortress, and strength, you know how weak and helpless and afraid we are in time of trouble. Protect us from the following temptations and dangers …

I Am the Lord Your God … a Jealous God

Invocation: Lord, you tell us that you are a jealous God. In the First Commandment you insist on being our only God. Be with us now as we think about why we serve only you.

Text: You shall have no other gods … for I, the Lord your God, am a jealous God. Ex. 20:3, 5

Insight: God is a jealous God, meaning he is so zealous about loving and about showing his love for his creatures that he will not tolerate sharing them (us) with any other supposed god. As recipients of that jealous, zealous love given to us through Jesus' death and resurrection we want to love him in return. We can call that "obedience," but it is not given grudgingly.

If your father or mother tells you as a child to do this or that and you don't, and if you then tell your father or mother that the reason you did not do what was commanded was because your friend told you didn't have to, what would your father or mother say? They would say, "What right does your friend have to advise you against our will? Are we not your parents? Don't we feed, protect, guide, educate, and keep you? You are responsible to us."

True, some parents might say that out of a misguided sense of ownership or ego, but not most parents. Their orders are given because they love their child and want only the best for him or her. They want the child to grow and to be able to love the parent even as the parent loves the child.

Because he loves us, God is the ideal parent. He does not want us to do what the world and Satan beckon us to do. As our Creator, Preserver, Redeemer, and Sanctifier, he cares about us and longs for us to join him in heaven.

Prayer: Dear Father, you have told us who you are through your Holy Word. Our subtle yet powerful false gods are … We know that we are not to have other gods, and we know that you insist on our obedience so that the false gods do not lead us to abandon you. Dear Father, give us the strength of your Holy Spirit especially against my false gods of …

WORSHIP IDEAS

Hymn Suggestions

"Blessed Be the Name"
"Father, I Adore You"
"Here Is the Tenfold Sure Command"
"Let Us Ever Walk with Jesus"
"We Worship You, O God of Might"
"Worthy, You Are Worthy"
"You Will I Love, My Strength"

Opening Sentences

Pastor: It is written: "Worship the Lord your God, and serve him only."

People: We will do everything the Lord has said.

Pastor: "You shall have no other gods before me."

People: We will fear, love, and trust only in God.

Confession of Sins

Pastor: The Lord our God has decreed, "Do not make any gods to be alongside me; do not make for yourselves gods of silver or gods of gold" (Ex. 20:23). Yet, people of God, our hearts and our deeds condemn us, for surely we have put our trust in ourselves, in our riches, and in our own resources. Therefore, let us confess our sinfulness and acknowledge wandering hearts.

All: O Lord, our God, we have sinned. We have failed to hold you above all the gods of our own creating. We have failed to trust you in all things and to turn to you in every need. We stand condemned, except for your great mercy and grace. Forgive us, renew us, and by your power enable us to cling to you alone. Amen.

Absolution

Pastor: You are forgiven. God has put away your sins. Now hear his gracious invitation: Whatever good thing you lack, look to me for it and seek it from me. Whenever you suffer misfortune or distress, come and cling to me. I am the one who will satisfy you and will help you out of every need. Therefore, let your heart cling only to me, for only I am able to satisfy the desires of every living thing.

People: Amen!

Scripture Readings

Lector: The fool says in his heart, "There is no God." They are corrupt, their deeds are vile; there is no one who does good (Ps. 14:1).

People: Whoever trusts in his riches will fall (Prov. 11:28).

Lector: You shall have no other gods before me (Ex. 20:3).

People: You shall not make for yourself an idol in the form of anything in heaven above or on the earth beneath or in the waters below. ... For I, the LORD your God, am a jealous God, punishing the children for the sins of the fathers to the third and fourth generation of those who hate me, but showing love to a thousand generations of those who love me and keep my commandments (Ex. 20:4–6).

Lector: Anyone who loves his father or mother more than me is not worthy of me; anyone who loves his son or daughter more than me is not worthy of me (Matt. 10:37).

People: Love the Lord your God with all your heart and with all your soul and with all your mind (Matt. 22:37).

TABLE CARD INSTRUCTIONS

How to use the table card:

1. Fold the card along the dotted lines to form a triangle. Staple, glue, or tape together.

2. Display for an effective reminder of this week's commandment and Scripture reference.

FOLD

I am the LORD your God.

First Commandment
You shall have no other gods before me.

FOLD

Praise be to the Lord, the God of Israel, because he has
come and has redeemed his people.
Luke 1:68

FOLD

THE SECOND COMMANDMENT

SERMON

O Lord, may the meditations of our hearts and the words of our mouths be acceptable to you, our Strength and our Redeemer. Amen.

Today we study the second commandment, "You shall not misuse the name of the LORD your God" (Ex. 20:7).

I'm afraid, my brothers and sisters, that the misuse of God's name is so rampant around us that it hardly even bothers us anymore. We used to be disturbed by it. I recall how shocked I was—and many other Christians were, too—when for the first time we saw the transcripts of President Nixon's tapes in that infamous time of Watergate. All the deleted expletives! I'm afraid that if our current president did the same thing, most of America today would yawn. We've come so far in accepting cursing and swearing in any kind of public arena that we hardly bat an eye. Go to a repair shop some late Saturday morning and listen to the frustration of those whose tools broke down before the job was finished. The only thing that would surprise you would be if there were no cursing.

Why are we not surprised? What's it going to take for us to have sensitive hearts again? What's it going to take for us to hold and revere the name of God and to honor it in such a way that those who are present with us know that we don't tolerate the misuse of the name of the Lord our God? What would it take to take seriously the commandment "You shall not misuse the name of the LORD your God"?

The answer to my question fills nearly every chapter of Scripture. When we know and appreciate all that God has done for us in spite of and because of our sins, we are too busy praising his name and too busy calling on his name for help—too much filled with his name—to have the time or desire to misuse it. We take it seriously, because the name of God stands for all that he is, all that he does, and all that he has promised to do for us.

Consider what happens inside you when you hear a person's name.

The phone rings; you pick it up and say "Hello." Then the other voice says, "Hello, I'm so-and-so."

If it's your friend, what happens? You say, "Well, hi! How are ya?" Your voice goes up; inside your mind you instantly envision that person, maybe the last time you were together. When the conversation is about something happy, you can picture the other person smiling; if it's something sad, you can almost see your friend's face. The name, you see, stands for the person.

If, however, that person on the phone is someone you don't like or with whom you're angry or a salesman, the name still conjures up a face—only now it turns your stomach into a knot. You can feel tension rise. The name, you see, stands for the person. And your response to that person is the same as your response to the name—and vice versa.

God has given to us his name—his holy name!—so that there can be a response of love and worship. When we hear the Holy name of God, the instant response is to be "Yes!" and, "This is my God, this is my Lord, this is my Savior." There is more to this commandment than simply using or misusing a name. In Hebrew, the picture is of lifting something up for all to see—honorably or otherwise. Later, the Levites would lift up the ark of the covenant and David would lift up psalms of praise. But for now, the people of God—those who had been taken up out of slavery and up through the waters that slew Pharaoh's army—were not only hearing God's own, personal name, *Yahweh,* they were also told, "Do not take my name as if it meant little. I give it to you to use, so that you can call upon me in the day of trouble, so that you know whom to thank for all the blessings of the day; so that you can ask for protection from all that goes bump in the night."

That is why God almost begs us in this commandment not to waste his name by misuse. If we frequently use his name so callously for no good reason, we soon will forget the power of that name when we really need it.

Some Christians who have used the name of the Lord in an inappropriate way give the excuse, "Oh, I really didn't mean anything with it." That's the problem.

The name of God can be properly used for cursing—for condemning the work of Satan. You should mean that curse, because there is a power in the name of God. By the same token, you are to use the name of God to bless. Why? Because it is the power of the Almighty. That's why the end of the service is so powerful. It's not a time to gather up our purse and close the bulletin. The benediction blessing is the powerful name of God, invoked upon the people of God, so that they can go out of church—and go with his might throughout the week. That's using God's powerful name. It carries his authority, and it works.

If you doubt that, think of the power of the most common name: *Mom.* The kids are down the hall in the playroom, and all of a sudden you hear them squabble. Oh, no! They're fighting again! You know what's going to happen next. One of them will come running and cry, "Mom, he just keeps hitting me!" And Mom will say, "You go tell your brother that I have said to quit fighting." Then the child will run down the hall—and what's the first thing you will hear? "*Mom* said!" Right?

The child will have gained power. How? By the name of *Mom.* You see? There is power in the name. How much more power exists in the name God has given to us, *his* name, so that it brings his power into the lives of those around.

Now, what is the name of God? It's in the original Hebrew commandment: You shall not misuse the name of *Yahweh,* your God. The name *Yahweh* is translated as "I AM" or "HE IS." " 'I AM.' That is my name. You can use it."

By the way, in some Bibles the word LORD in the Old Testament sometimes is capitalized—not just the first letter, but all the letters. That indicates that the Hebrew word there is God's personal name: *Yahweh.* That indicates that this is not just any god who is speaking or acting, but it is *Yahweh,* the God who chose Abraham, Isaac, Jacob, all of Israel, who created the universe—this is who we're talking about.

The New Testament may not use the word *Yahweh,* but Jesus lets us know that he himself is the "I AM." Think of the many different titles of the "I AM" Jesus used for himself. I am the way, the truth, and the life. I am the bread of life. I am the door, the gate. I am the light of the world. I am the vine, you are the branches. I am the good shepherd. I am the resurrection and the life. I am the Son of God.

There is power in knowing that he is the way, the truth, and the life. There is power in knowing that in him only, in his name, is salvation. There is power in knowing that when you are troubled with your sin, he is your salvation. "There is no other name under heaven given to men by which we must be saved" (Acts 4:12). There is power in the fact that Sunday after Sunday a pastor stands up in front of you and, in the name of the Father and of the Son and of the Holy Spirit, absolves you of all of your sins.

There is power in the fact that he says, "The Father will give you whatever you ask in my name" (John 15:16).

That's God giving to you his name.

There is power, my brothers and sisters, in the name God has given to us. The name, the great "I AM." That's why we hold it precious. That's why we do not misuse it. We revere the name of Jesus; we don't want to misuse it. We don't want to take it lightly. We don't want ever to use it as if it means nothing at all. No—we treasure it! We love it! We honor it! That is why we claim for ourselves the Gospel meaning of this commandment: Because God has redeemed us, we will call upon his name in every trouble, pray, praise, and give him thanks.

In the *name* of the Father and of the Son and of the Holy Spirit. Amen.

This Is My Name

Invocation: In the name of the Father and of the Son and of the Holy Spirit. Amen.

Text: God said to Moses, "I AM WHO I AM. ... This is my name forever, the name by which I am to be remembered from generation to generation. Ex. 3:14, 15

Insight: Selecting a name for a newborn is an exciting, challenging task. Family and friends are surveyed for suggestions and opinions. Finally a decision is reached. The infant receives a name that it will bear—proudly or otherwise—for its lifetime.

God declared his own name. He stated that he is the "I AM." He declared so to Moses and the Israelites; then in the New Testament, he gave his name a face—Jesus Christ. His very name describes who he is. It stands for his deity, his righteousness, his perfectness, his eternity.

To acknowledge this "I AM" is not merely a casual comment that he is our Lord and Savior. Rather, it is a sincere conviction, Spirit-given, that this God is truly the Lord of the universe, in whom all power, truth, and knowledge reside.

God's name itself calls us to submit to his lordship over all. In his holiness he does not wink at our sin. He hates it. But in his perfect love, he covers that sin with the blood of Christ. And the power of his name enables us to do all that he asks.

Prayer: You are my Lord and my Savior. Fill me with your Spirit so that I may ...

Power in Praising

Invocation: In the name of the Father and of the Son and of the Holy Spirit. Amen.

Text: Glorify the LORD with me; let us exalt his name together. Ps. 34:3

Insight: "Fabulous dinner, Mom."

"Your report is excellent—an A for you."

"You handled that client perfectly."

Words of praise—we thrive on them. Compliments put smiles on our faces. Recognition of creative, successful work motivates us to continue. Any parent or teacher will tell you that rewards for good behavior produce happy children and a pleasant atmosphere.

Praising God, however, is a different matter. We do not assume that he has forgotten how great he is. Nor does he need our praise in order to make him creative or pleasant to be around. We praise him because *we* need the reminders of his worth, his mercy, his forgiveness in Jesus, his strength in us, his grace.

What a wonderful way to use God's name—to praise him. Try it during your private meditation. Finish this sentence as many ways as possible: "God, you are as great as _____." Or think of your own praise sentence to complete.

There is power in praising. We are strengthened in our faith as we remember his many daily acts of mercy toward us. All our humble expressions of praise are received by our gracious God. He accepts them and continues to bless us in our worship.

Prayer: Lord, may your praise be continually in our heart and on our lips. Enable us to praise you by ...

A Glorious and Awesome God

Invocation: In the name of the Father and of the Son and of the Holy Spirit. Amen.

Text: Revere this glorious and awesome name—the LORD your God. Deut. 28:58

Insight: Consider some situation that could be described as awesome. Would it be the California Angels winning the World Series; humans walking on the moon; a sunset? To some, *awesome* describes the flying buttresses of Notre Dame or the immense altar in St. Peter's. The adjective *awesome* is used in describing unusual, superhuman deeds or persons.

Whatever other picture comes to mind at mention of the word, it must also refer to our God. He belongs to a time and space that mortals cannot fully comprehend. No human can completely fathom the mysteries of God. What a wonderful truth that is!

Far greater yet is the fact that this omnipotent God came to earth in human form to be our brother and our Savior. As the God-Man, he understands our every need, fear, and feeling. He goes beyond just understanding; he acts. Daily he intervenes in our lives to work out his plan for us. His care and concern for us extend to the most secret part of our being.

Our prayers are important to him, and he always listens, always answers. This awesome God loves each child whom he has called to be his own.

Therefore, we pray in the glorious, powerful name of Jesus in full confidence that the God who caused Mount Sinai to tremble also lovingly soothes every hurt and calms every fear. That indeed is awesome!

Prayer: Glorious Lord, assure me of your loving care, especially when ...

His Name Is Holy

Invocation: In the name of the Father and of the Son and of the Holy Spirit. Amen.

Text: For this is what the high and lofty One says—he who lives forever, whose name is holy. Is. 57:15

Insight: The blue lights were flashing as I finally glanced into my rearview mirror. I knew what the officer would say before I rolled down my window: "Do you know what you did when you made that left turn?" His explanation was unnecessary. I knew it was wrong, but ... I'd seen so many others do it. If they do it, why can't I?

Breaking a traffic rule made me feel stupid and cost me $104. That's such a small thing in the total picture of life. However, my underlying motive for my traffic infraction is not so small. I do wrong things merely because others do. Is that true for you also?

The holiness of God's name is a tenet that I've known since childhood. Yet, sadly enough, phrases that carelessly use his precious name also slip out of my mouth. Although I hear it in the media or from co-workers, my excuses are nonexistent. I know it's wrong. I do it anyway. That constant battle is waged daily within me and within the heart of every Christian.

The weapon for winning that war is also ours. It's the power of the Spirit, given to us in God's own Word. The sins of our mouth are forgiven and forgotten by a gracious Savior, who gave his life so that our lips might speak of his wonders and proclaim his glory.

Prayer: Precious Jesus, my heart is filled with thanks for your forgiveness of all my sin, but especially for forgiving me ...

WORSHIP IDEAS

Hymn Suggestions

"Blessed Be the Name"
"Glorify Thy Name"
"His Name Is Wonderful"
"How Majestic Is Your Name"
"Jesus, Name Above All Names"
"Praise the Name of Jesus"

Opening Sentences

Pastor: Welcome, people of God. Welcome into the house of the Lord. We have gathered for the most sacred time of the week. God comes to us, and we in turn respond with worship and praise.

People: May the words of our mouths and the meditations of our hearts be acceptable to you, O Lord, our Rock and our Redeemer.

Pastor: In the strong name of our God, Father, Son, and Holy Spirit.

People: Amen.

Pastor: Worship the Lord with gladness. Come before him with joyful songs.

People: We know that the Lord is good. He made us and we are his people.

Pastor: Enter into his palace with thanksgiving and into his house with praise.

People: We will give thanks to him and praise his name. His faithfulness continues through all generations.

Confession of Sins

Pastor: The Lord spoke: "You shall not misuse the name of the Lord your God, for the Lord will not hold anyone guiltless who misuses his name." It is a misuse of God's name when we use it in any way whatsoever to support falsehood or wrong of any kind. It is a misuse of his name to take it up as our name on Sundays and then for our lives to deny it the rest of the week.

Truly we are all guilty and stand before the Lord as violators of this commandment. Let us acknowledge our wrongdoing and seek his pardon and peace.

All: We have misused your name, O God. We acknowledge that though your name is powerful, we have used it flippantly and even as if it were meaningless. We stand guilty. We also stand repentant. Forgive us and cleanse our lips that we might use your name to pray and praise, to witness, and to give thanks.

Absolution

Pastor: It is in using the name of the Lord our God and the power that is contained in it that I proclaim to you the forgiveness of all your sins: You are pardoned in the name of the Father and of the Son and of the Holy Spirit. Amen.

Scripture Readings

Lector: God said to Moses, "I AM WHO I AM."

People: This is what you are to say to the Israelites: "I AM has sent me to you" (Ex. 3:14).

Lector: I am the LORD, that is my name! I will not give my glory to another or my praise to idols (Is. 42:8).

People: You shall not misuse the name of the LORD your God, for the LORD will not hold anyone guiltless who misuses his name (Ex. 20:7).

Lector: If anyone curses his God, he will be held responsible (Lev. 24:15).

People: With the tongue we praise our Lord and Father, and with it we curse men, who have been made in God's likeness. Out of the same mouth come praise and cursing. My brothers, this should not be (James 3:9–10).

Lector: Fear the LORD your God, serve him only and take your oaths in his name (Deut. 6:13).

People: Where two or three come together in my name, there am I with them (Matt. 18:20).

Lector: God exalted [Jesus] to the highest place and gave him the name that is above every name,

People: That at the name of Jesus every knee should bow, in heaven and on earth and under the earth, and every tongue confess that Jesus Christ is Lord, to the glory of God the Father (Phil. 2:9–11).

Lector: Go and make disciples of all nations, baptizing them in the name of the Father and of the Son and of the Holy Spirit (Matt. 28:19).

People: My Father will give you whatever you ask in my name (John 16:23).

TABLE CARD INSTRUCTIONS

How to use the table card:

1. Fold the card along the dotted lines to form a triangle. Staple, glue, or tape together.
2. Display for an effective reminder of this week's commandment and Scripture reference.

.... FOLD

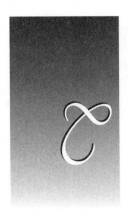

Let us exalt the name of our glorious God.

Second Commandment

You shall not misuse the name of the LORD your God.

.... FOLD

My Father will give you whatever you ask in my name.

John 16:23

.... FOLD

THE THIRD COMMANDMENT

SERMON

In the blessed name of our God, Father, Son, and Holy Spirit. Amen.

Before I read the Third Commandment and the verses that go with it, I need to read the prelude to this, from Gen. 2:2–3, so that when we read the commandment, we will see it in the light of these words:

> By the seventh day God had finished the work he had been doing; so on the seventh day he rested from all his work. And God blessed the seventh day and made it holy, because on it he rested from all the work of creating that he had done.

Now today's text, Ex. 20:8–11:

> Remember the Sabbath day by keeping it holy. Six days you shall labor and do all your work, but the seventh day is a Sabbath to the LORD your God. On it you shall not do any work, neither you, nor your son or daughter, nor your manservant or maidservant, nor your animals, nor the alien within your gates. For in six days the LORD made the heavens and the earth, the sea, and all that is in them, but he rested on the seventh day. Therefore the LORD blessed the Sabbath day and made it holy.

What a day that very first Saturday must have been! God looking over what he had created. The creation stretching out before him—sea and land, plants and animals, stars, sun and moon, galaxies—all stretching out before him. So he sits down and relaxes. And he looks over everything that he has done and reflects about having done it.

Have you ever done that? Maybe it was a landscaping project that you had around your house. Maybe it was a creative piece of needlework. Maybe you decided to redo an old automobile. Or maybe it was finally having signed a major contract at your business. Then you sat back and relaxed. Maybe a friend was with you, maybe your spouse, maybe a co-worker, maybe you had a glass of iced tea in your hand. You reflected on and enjoyed what you had done, the work of your hand.

What was going through the mind of God after he had finished and was reflecting on it all? I think it was something like this: "Now I can rest. I finished my work for the week, and it's really great. My Word was powerful; it accomplished everything that I wanted it to. Now I can sit back and reflect upon the joy of doing that. Ah, this is good. Hey! This is so good that I think I'm going to give that same kind of gift to the people whom I've created, because I've given them the ability to be able to work and to create things and to accomplish things. I know what I'm going to do: I'm going to make it a commandment that on this particular day, once every week, they will just sit back and relax and enjoy what they have done—and enjoy me, the one who gave them the capacity to work. And they can reflect upon my graciousness to them and on our relationship with each other."

That's the kind of thing I think God said that day. That's really the spirit that is behind this third commandment. As God said in another setting in which he repeated his commandments, "Observe my Sabbaths and have reverence for my sanctuary" (Lev. 19:30). The Sabbath was given to us as a gift, as a way to reflect on all God has done for us and a way to give ourselves to that which is the most fundamental to any relationship: communication.

The bare words of the commandment in Exodus 20 do not explicitly say anything about communication, about Bible reading, prayer, and worship. The thought of Lev. 19:30, "have reverence for my sanctuary," is there, however, in the verb *remember*. God remembered Noah in the ark and, therefore, did something about it by drying up the waters. God then promised to always remember—and keep—the covenant to never flood the whole earth again. When Sodom and Gomorrah were destroyed, God remembered Abraham and therefore saved Lot and his family. Two generations later, we are told that God remembered Rachel and opened her womb to the birth of Joseph and later Benjamin. Some 400 years later God remembered his promises to Abraham, Isaac, and Jacob—and so brought Israel out of Egypt.

Remember? Yes—by doing something about what you remember.

And what is it you are to remember? The Sabbath day, that is, the end day (for that is what *Sabbath* means: "the end, the ceasing"). But there are three end times to remember: the ceasing of God's original act of creation; the weekly ceasing from our own work in memory of God's ceasing; and especially the ceasing of the rule of sin in the world with the arrival of God in the flesh, Jesus the Christ, and Jesus' ultimate arrival on the Day of Judgment.

Now, that's something to remember!

For the Old Testament believers, "remembering" the future end meant waiting for the coming of the Messiah—who was expected to arrive on an end day, a Sabbath day. And he would bring the ultimate rest: peace with God and with all creation. Sin and its consequences would be removed. When he would arrive, even mortal enemies such as lambs and wolves could relax next to each other.

So when Jesus came, he was called our Sabbath rest, the one to whom the commandment pointed. Thus Jesus could say that the Lord of the Sabbath is here, and he could work on Saturday and do miracles. And the disciples could thresh a little bit on Saturday and pop the kernels into their mouths. You see?

You and I, therefore, no longer have to live under the literal impact of this commandment, not working on the seventh day. However, the command behind the command, the basic injunction that we remember—in word and action—what God did the days before he ceased creating the universe and what God did to call a halt to the rule of Satan in our hearts—that command to honor God still stands. He is still the foundation of our physical as well as our spiritual life. All this we know and believe—and grow stronger in believing and living—only because of and through God's own Word.

Remember when Jesus told the story of two men; one of whom built his house upon a rock and the other on sand? Perhaps you have seen TV news coverage or photos of people who build gorgeous sand castles on the beaches of California. How those imagined and fantasy castles are admired! Judges even award prizes. But what happens to those sand castles after the prize is awarded? The tide comes in, and they return to being beach—little particles of silicon and barely even a memory.

People are like that. Those who despise the Word of God and want to build a life apart from God and his instructions about our lives are like that. Oh, man, can they build some beautiful lives! Other people begin to admire them, and some even get the prizes of riches and fame. But if they have not built their lives on the Word of God, they are only sand castles. One day they too will only be specks of dirt, a granite slab for only a few generations.

When we examine ourselves under this command, we have to admit that although we may have tried to keep this commandment, we have not built our lives *perfectly* upon it. Once again, the Law comes to us and serves as a mirror to show us our sins—so that, seeing we are not what we ought to be, we get down on our knees, forsake righteousness in our own self, and turn to Jesus for forgiveness. And that's exactly what he gives: our ultimate Sabbath rest, and we are grateful to be in the loving and protecting arms of God.

When you hear that, do you think, "Well, why don't I just ignore the commandment? If it's all been fulfilled, and if I'm covered in the blood of Jesus for it and don't have to be afraid of the punishment or think I have to win God's favor, then why don't I just forget about this 'Remember the Sabbath day'?"

You know what the response is, don't you? Because Jesus has fulfilled it for us, we seek to honor God out of love, not fear. We reverence his sanctuary because church is the place we set aside (make holy) to celebrate the presence of God among us and to worship him.

So now we ask the question, "*How* do we keep the Sabbath day holy?" By hearing the Word of God as it is preached and by listening to it deeply and reverently—and then by setting forth to do the Word of God in every day of our lives. That can happen because the Word of God is a power-filled Word. That same creative Word of God that caused all the world to come into being in the day of creation now goes to work inside of us. And what does it create? It creates faith, and it creates trust, and it creates love. And then it creates a desire for us to be obedient to God and to his Word. And the reading of the Word of God creates in us fear, love, and trust in God and causes us to want to desire that Word even more. It's a self-perpetuating cycle, if you will.

As a result, the author of the letter to the Hebrews encourages us, "Let us consider how we may spur one another on toward love and good deeds. Let us not give up meeting together, as some are in the habit of doing, but let us encourage one another—and all the more as you see the Day approaching" (Heb. 10:24–25).

There it says we are to encourage each other to assemble together in worship. Although we would never discourage private worship and the study of God's Word, he has urged his family to come together and corporately worship—to encourage each other in our prayers and in our singing, together to hear his Word and to encourage each other to be obedient to it. This is part of God's design.

I have known about people who have come to a certain spot in nature and have been so overcome by its beauty or majesty that words of praise easily leap full-blown from their heart. But some of those same people also describe an incredible loneliness, as if an emptiness has entered into their soul when they suddenly realize that there are no other people of God with them to share this moment. No one to pray with, no one to sing with.

We need each other Sunday after Sunday here in the house of the Lord, so that we might be able to encourage one another in keeping that Word of God sacred, hearing it, learning it, and doing it.

Therefore, let us remember the Sabbath day and keep holy this gift of rest in the resurrection, rest from the guilt of sin, rest from having to try to earn salvation or to fear punishment, rest that we might reflect upon God, rest for our bodies as well as for our souls. Amen.

The Day of Rest

Invocation: In the name of the Father and of the Son and of the Holy Spirit. Amen.

Text: God blessed the seventh day and made it holy, because on it he rested from all the work of creating that he had done. Gen. 2:3

Insight: After I've done something creative (by my standards at any rate), I enjoy looking over what I've accomplished. It makes me feel good. I imagine God felt very good on the seventh day when "he rested from all the work of creating that he had done."

God put aside a special day—a nonlabor day—to celebrate. What do we do to make a day special? Go on a family outing? Go shopping? Read a book? Or? God made this day special by declaring the day holy—a holy day. The Bible doesn't tell us how God celebrated, only that he rested. Maybe the angels and all the company of heaven had a lot of fun together praising in song the triune God for the magnificent creation.

We have the opportunity to celebrate with God every Sunday (at the very least). Sundays can be a day of rest for us, but God wants us to remember what this holy day is *really* about: acknowledging his work, not ours.

Fortunately, when we do falter and worship God as an afterthought, he forgives us and never holds our sins against us. We are to rest on the Sabbath, but not be lazy in our worship of the Mighty Creator. God loves us and wants us to join together in his house with the joyful and loving hearts of forgiven people.

Prayer: Lord God, heavenly Father, we praise and thank you for this great creation of yours. Today we especially praise you for …

Keeping a Holy Day

Invocation: In the name of the Father and of the Son and of the Holy Spirit. Amen.

Text: Since, then, you have been raised with Christ, set your hearts on things above, where Christ is seated at the right hand of God. Set your minds on things above, not on earthly things. Col. 3:1–2

Insight: A few facts I picked up from these verses:

- Jesus arose!
- He sits beside God in a place of honor and power!
- The triune God is in control!
- We are to think of things above! We are not to worry about things here on earth.

No matter how hard I try not to worry, sometimes I still do—and it's usually when I'm trying to have control of my life rather than allowing God to take control of it. We are not to worry, because we believe that Jesus Christ is the Son of God. Sounds simple enough, but … Sometimes, I think if I worry enough, something bad won't happen—or maybe the bad will go away. Sound familiar? *Control* is the key word here.

Worrying is such a waste of our precious time here on earth—*big* waste of time! Can we change anything by worry? Of course not! Our Lord is in charge, and he tells us to fill our thoughts with something more important—something such as what really is in store for us: heaven! With our minds and hearts free from worry, we can keep every day holy. And when we falter, we are assured of God's forgiveness—which again makes every day a holy-day.

Prayer: O holy Lord, forgive me when I worry. Help me to give these troubles to you, because you have promised to never forsake me …

Gladly Hear and Learn It

Invocation: In the name of the Father and of the Son and of the Holy Spirit. Amen.

Text: Blessed rather are those who hear the word of God and obey it. Luke 11:28

Insight: The Third Commandment is clear about hearing the Word of God, studying the Word of God, and trusting the Word of God. We need to do these things so that we can always be alert to temptations and more readily fight them.

The message of Luke 11:28 is that we are blessed when we hear God's Word. Right? Wrong! The big word in this passage is *and*. We are blessed if we hear *and* put it into practice/obey it.

It is one thing for a teacher to tell students the importance of staying off drugs, but quite another if that same teacher doesn't obey those words in his or her own life.

We hear God's Word on the Sabbath; we receive the forgiveness we all long for; and when we leave the house of the Lord, we want to put into practice all that we've heard—including the forgiveness part. God expects us to try to be good, but thankfully, he forgives us when we fail. Therefore, we gladly return Sunday after Sunday to hear the Word, learn from it, and with God's help, put it into practice.

Prayer: Lord, thank you for your Word and forgiveness. Help me …

Holding the Word Sacred

Invocation: In the name of the Father and of the Son and of the Holy Spirit. Amen.

Text: And we also thank God continually because, when you received the word of God, which you heard from us, you accepted it not as the word of men, but as it actually is, the word of God, which is at work in you who believe. 1 Thess. 2:13

Insight: "I won't believe everything your child says happens at home, if you won't believe everything he/she says happens at school." Teachers often make this comment to parents, because children (as well as adults), tend to get things mixed up. We have all learned not to believe everything we hear or read.

As Christians, we can always be sure of one thing: the Holy Word of our triune God, which he gave for us to learn. As Paul says, "The Word of God … is at work in you who believe."

Accepting the Word of God as truth means trusting it, and trust leads to peace. Proof of this fact is all around us. Think how peaceless you would be if you did not trust most people to drive on the right side of the road, or did not trust the floor joists in your house.

With complete trust in God's Word, we have complete peace in him. As a result, our lives change. We face each day knowing that our Lord is always with us, making each day holy.

Prayer: Thank you, God, for your Word! Help me to get rid of the things that worry me just now …

WORSHIP IDEAS

Hymn Suggestions

"Thy Strong Word"

"O Word of God Incarnate"

"How Precious Is the Book Divine"

"Majesty"

"Thy Word"

"Almighty God, Your Word Is Cast"

"O Day of Rest and Gladness"

Opening Sentences

Pastor: In the name of the triune God, Father, Son, and Holy Spirit, the Lord of creation and the Lord of each day, who gives us both labor and rest and who renews us through his Word.

People: Amen.

Pastor: You are gathered to sanctify this holy day. This day was created for rest and for worship. It is a day on which we follow the example of the early Christians, of whom it is said, "They devoted themselves to the apostles' teaching and to the fellowship, to the breaking of bread and to prayer" (Acts 2:42).

People: We are gathered to remember the Sabbath day by keeping it holy. We dedicate ourselves to being filled today with the encouragement of the Word of God, to hear it and to learn it.

Pastor: Let us, then, sing of our God, who creates, sustains, loves, and forgives us. Let us encourage each other to deep devotion and praise.

Confession of Sins

Pastor: When do we sin against this commandment?

People: We sin against this commandment when we choose to neglect the Word of God, when we do not honor the physical life he created or the spiritual life created in his Son. We sin against this commandment when we assume he will never come again to judge this day as holy.

Pastor: Are we guilty of any of these?

People: Yes, we are guilty of these and seek the forgiveness of God for Jesus' sake. We also seek more diligent hearts and more obedient lives to the holy Word of God.

Absolution

Pastor: Our holy God, who is the Word and who speaks through the Word, has spoken words of forgiveness and love through his Son, Jesus, our Lord. He who forgives you also sanctifies you, that you might be a holy people unto him, dedicated to hearing and keeping his Word.

People: Praise the name of Jesus. Amen.

Scripture Readings

Lector: Remember the Sabbath day by keeping it holy. … For in six days the LORD made the heavens and the earth, the sea, and all that is in them, but he rested on the seventh day. Therefore the LORD blessed the Sabbath day and made it holy (Ex. 20:8, 11).

People: I love the house where you live, O LORD, the place where your glory dwells (Ps. 26:8).

Lector: A time is coming and has now come when the true worshipers will worship the Father in spirit and truth, for they are the kind of worshipers the Father seeks. God is spirit, and his worshipers must worship in spirit and in truth (John 4:23–24).

People: Do not let anyone judge you by what you eat or drink, or with regard to a religious festival, a New Moon celebration or a Sabbath day. These are a shadow of things that were to come; the reality, however, is found in Christ (Col. 2:16–17).

Lector: One man considers one day more sacred than another; another man considers every day alike. Each one should be fully convinced in his own mind. He who regards one day as special, does it to the Lord …

People: For none of us lives to himself alone and none of us dies to himself alone. If we live, we live to the Lord; and if we die, we die to the Lord. So, whether we live or die, we belong to the Lord. For this very reason, Christ died and returned to life so that he might be the Lord of both the dead and the living (Rom. 14:5–9).

All: Let us consider how we may spur one another on toward love and good deeds. Let us not give up meeting together, as some are in the habit of doing, but let us encourage one another—and all the more as you see the Day approaching (Heb. 10:24).

How to use the table card:

1. Fold the card along the dotted lines to form a triangle. Staple, glue, or tape together.
2. Display for an effective reminder of this week's commandment and Scripture reference.

FOLD

21We will gladly hear and learn your Word.

Third Commandment
Remember the Sabbath day by keeping it holy.

FOLD

Let the word of Christ dwell in you richly as you teach and admonish one another with all wisdom, and as you sing psalms, hymns and spiritual songs with gratitude in your hearts to God.

Col. 3:16

FOLD

THE FOURTH COMMANDMENT

SERMON

Grace, mercy and peace, in the name of our triune God: the Father, the Son, and the Holy Spirit. Amen.

The Word of God for today is the Fourth Commandment, Ex. 20:12: "Honor your father and your mother, so that you may live long in the land the LORD your God is giving you."

Luther says something really quite remarkable, it seems to me, about this particular commandment. In his Large Catechism he wrote, "We know that [keeping this commandment] is highly pleasing to the divine Majesty and all the angels, that it vexes all devils, and, besides, that it is the greatest work that we can do, next to the sublime worship of God described in the previous commandments" (LC I 125).

When was the last time that you tried to think about what you might do that would absolutely be a good work before God, something that would truly honor him? In fact, have you ever tried even to think of the most noble good work that you could possibly do before God? And if you did, did you conclude that that good work would be to honor and respect your mom and dad? I don't think most people would conclude that. They might choose as the highest good work being a missionary in some third-world country or a CEO in some great Christian company or being the ideal president of the United States, but I don't think many people would have said, "As the best good work on earth, I'll honor my mom and dad."

Luther based his comment on a number of factors. First, God's second table of the Law, how we are to deal with others on this earth, leads off with God's call to honor parents, implying thereby the commandment's high status. Second, this is the only commandment regarding human relationships that gives a specific about what we should do rather than the generic prohibitions of the other commandments. "Don't steal," for example, doesn't say what we *should* do instead. In the Fourth Commandment, however, God is quite explicit. Third, although love is the fulfillment of the Law (Rom. 13:10), honor is higher than love because it includes love along with respect, deference, and humility. Fourth, the fact that this is the only commandment with a promised blessing attests to the high value God places on the concern. Fifth, in honoring one's parents, God is including our duty to honor all authority. All authority established in this world comes from God.

What's most amazing is that, with rare exception, God's authority is channeled through the family. It's like a delta. It springs from this one source, the commandment, into the whole community. That's why we can call our political leaders our civic fathers. It's a family term. The same idea holds true about teachers and employers. Their authority too flows out of the family and ultimately from God. That explains why lawlessness breaks out most openly where the family is weakest or nonexistent. That's why it's so important that schools and families cooperate together in the instruction and rearing of children.

Perhaps at this point you're thinking that some parents and others in authority do not deserve to be honored. It's true—some are rascals; that's all there's to it. But the exception does not make the rule. We'd all admit that it is pretty tough being a parent sometimes. You can't always, for example, be patient. I'm reminded of this young dad who was wheeling a shopping cart through the grocery store with his screaming little child in it. As he was going down the aisle, people heard him saying, "It's okay, Freddy. You are going to make it, Freddy. Just calm down; it's going to be okay. In about 10 minutes at the most we're going to be home." A lady who overheard this walked up to him and said, "I must compliment you on how patient you are with young Freddy." The man replied, "Thanks, but I'm Freddy."

On a much more serious level, some parents are abusive to their children and cause scars that last a lifetime. There is no excuse for this. None. Nevertheless, the existence of bad parents does not change that God calls us to honor and respect those who are in authority over us. If you are stopped by a police officer for speeding and the officer acts rude while writing out a ticket, you nevertheless better honor the office or you're going to have a whole lot more difficulty than just paying a ticket. You see, one is to respect the office, even if the one who is in it is not fulfilling it and doing what he or she should.

Every one of us has to admit that we've got something to repent of. None of us have lived perfectly. We have not perfectly honored our parents, our employees, our government officials (including our president). Therefore, we are called to repent, to seek forgiveness.

What do you do if you have guilt? For example, maybe you are mindful of some disrespect to a parent who has now died. What can you do about that? Many people are going to therapists these days and bleeding out their lives about a child or about their parents and the hurt that they are feeling. They will not be healed if all they're doing is casting blame on their parents or someone else. Likewise, wallowing in one's own guilt cures nothing. Only forgiveness has that power; for when you receive forgiveness, then you are able also to give it to others. And only then can healing start. Only then is there hope.

That's tough to do. I think of those who have parents or children who simply refuse to give or receive love. No hugs. Not even kind words. Sometimes not even basic politeness in lieu of love. Nothing unless it's bitterness. How can a person give forgiveness and love if it's rejected?

That's when we need to focus on God's forgiveness and love. He knows well what it is like when love is rejected. But it is the nature of love that it can only be offered and never forced. God has given his love to the world, but he doesn't force it. That is the heart of God.

The perfection God would like to see in us is seen by him in the life of his Son, Jesus. He was obedient not only to Mary and Joseph (Luke 2:51), he was obedient to his heavenly Father's command to take the guilt and punishment for our sins to the cross. Just as his punishment has replaced ours, so his righteous life has become ours in the Father's eyes. As a result, with his life now our life, empowering us, we offer forgiveness and love even to those who do not deserve it. And because we honor the eternal Father, we honor his representatives of authority among us— if not for their persons, then for their office. This we do in the name of the Father and the Son and the Holy Spirit. Amen.

Parents Are God's Servants

Invocation: In the name of the Father and of the Son and of the Holy Spirit. Amen.

Text: For he is God's servant to do you good. Rom. 13:4

Insight: The dictionary defines a parent as one that begets or brings forth offspring. What an incomplete definition! God, our Father, knows that being a parent—a proper and Christian parent—requires more. It means serving your children to do them good (to use the terms in the text). Parents and all in authority exist to protect, benefit, and nurture those in their care.

God wants us to take our responsibilities seriously. But we don't always do that. Too often we put our own wants and desires before the needs of those we serve. Why? Because we still are too much like children; we want to be the ones being served; we want our own desires met; we are (to be brutally honest) self-centered and selfish.

Thank God that he is not as we are. He sent his Son as the ultimate servant, the Suffering Servant as described by Isaiah as "pierced for our transgressions" and "crushed for our iniquities" so that "by his wounds we are healed" (Is. 53:5). Because he has so served us, we now know how to and are able to be servants of his—willing servants. And we gratefully accept the responsibility he has given us to be his representative to our children, preparing them also to go into the world as responsible Christians.

Prayer: Dear Father, praise to you for renewing time and again your covenant by placing in our midst your beautiful children. Give us strength as parents and children to serve you well as we …

God Establishes Authority

Invocation: In the name of the Father and of the Son and of the Holy Spirit. Amen.

Text: Everyone must submit himself to the governing authorities, for there is no authority except that which God has established. Rom. 13:1

Insight: "Submit? Give in? Me? No way! Not to that so-and-so."

Have you had that thought a time or two? Who was it about, a boss? a pastor? a teacher? a parent?

Submission is tough. Why? Because we know more than anybody else, of course.

Take my father, also my boss for 10 years in our family business. Each morning I was given my marching orders. Then he and I would do battle. My comments: "Why this way? This makes no sense. I'm not going to do it!" Sometimes I'd threaten to quit. Sometimes I'd give in and do it his way. Sometimes I'd do it my way. And do you know what? In the end it really didn't make much difference. What mattered was that my rebellion caused hurt, discord, and guilt in our family that lasted for years.

The Deut. 5:16 version of the commandment to honor parents adds the promise "that it may go well with you." How sad that I took so long in learning that God had my best interests at heart! The hurt I caused was felt not only by my father but by me, too, as well as others in the family.

Were it not for Jesus, I would have to go to the grave guilty and unforgiven. But when Pilate sentenced Jesus to death, our Lord submitted—for my sake, for your sake. And we are forgiven.

I cannot relive or change my years of rebellion, but I can move forward, living a changed life, because the power of God lives in me. Thanks be to God, who gives us the victory through Jesus!

Prayer: Praise to you Father, Authority of all authorities. I thank you for forgiving my rebellion against …

If Respect, Then Respect

Invocation: In the name of the Father and of the Son and of the Holy Spirit. Amen.

Text: Give everyone what you owe him ... if respect, then respect. Rom. 13:7

Insight: Our friend Tom became a teacher at age 20. He wanted very badly to be respected.

"Don't crack a smile until Christmas," was the advice of his headmaster. "In this way you will earn the respect of your students."

Tom, a good and compassionate man, found out the hard way about respect. By Christmas, he was roundly hated by his students. Determined to find out if teaching was to be his career, he decided to drop the "cold efficiency" act and be himself. His genuine goodness, humor, and compassion was winning. Within weeks his students had gained great respect for him.

God does not set us up for failure; he wants us to succeed. It is our own desires that lead us astray. Yet time and time again, God forgives.

Each of us has special talents the Lord our God has given us, things that we are good at, things that come naturally. He has given us the ability to know what is good and what is not and the right to choose. And because his Spirit lives in our hearts, we are able to choose well.

Prayer: Father, we praise you for being all-compassionate. Forgive us as we strive for respect while sometimes choosing not to respect the Most Holy One. Especially ...

If Honor, Then Honor

Invocation: In the name of the Father and of the Son and of the Holy Spirit. Amen.

Text: Give everyone what you owe him ... if honor, then honor. Rom. 13:7

Insight: I'm sure that you can recall many a time—a luncheon, a dinner, an assembly—when you bestowed honors upon some deserving individual. The fact that anybody does that is remarkable, for it is a time when we go against our human nature. People would rather acclaim themselves. Our Father, in our text, tells us to do what is humanly unnatural but is natural in the new life given by God's Spirit.

Note the preface to the call to honor a person: "Give everyone what you owe him." The context implies that the "everyone" may well be someone in authority, someone you don't know personally, someone who on a human level is not worthy of honor. In spite of that God enjoins us to honor those to whom honor is *owed* by virtue of who or what they are.

All this because "there is no authority except that which God has established" (13:1).

The reason for such honor is not necessarily a great job done but a great God behind the person to whom honor is owed. That God—our God—has chosen to bless us through representative authority. Therefore, when we honor these people, we are honoring the God who has redeemed us by his Son and who serves us with his love.

Prayer: Praise and honor to you, Father. Thank you for forgiving my failure to know those whom you have appointed to serve me. Today, Father, ...

WORSHIP IDEAS

Hymn Suggestions

"Give Us Homes"
"Happy the Home When God Is There"
"Make Me a Servant"
"Oh, Blest the House"
"Our Father, by Whose Name"
"The Man Is Ever Blessed"

Opening Sentences

Pastor: The blessed Word of God says, "There is no authority except that which God has established. The authorities that exist have been established by God" (Rom. 13:1). Today we affirm the authority of God and that which he has placed in the home, nation, and church. Let us make a confession of faith based on the Fourth Commandment.

People: We believe in God the Father Almighty, Maker of heaven and earth, who governs us through his Word and through the authorities he has placed over us. We hear his word: "Honor your father and your mother, so that you may live long in the land the LORD your God is giving you."

Confession of Sins

Pastor: Let us confess our sins and failures to God, our dear Father.

All: We confess to you, O Father, that we have not always respected and honored those in authority over us. We have often rebelled against our parents and employers, our government officials and our spiritual leaders. In so doing, we acknowledge that we are in rebellion against you, for all authority is given by you. For Jesus' sake, forgive us this our sin and enable us to honor those you set above us. We pray in Jesus' name. Amen.

Absolution

Pastor: "Take heart, sons and daughters," our Lord says, "your sins are forgiven" (Matt. 9:2). Our Father in heaven has given his beloved Son so that we receive the forgiveness of all our sins. He also has given his Holy Spirit to strengthen us so that we might learn to be obedient to him and to those he gives to us to honor and obey. Live, then, in his grace and love.

People: Amen.

Scripture Readings

Lector: I will send you the prophet Elijah before that great and dreadful day of the LORD comes. He will turn the hearts of the fathers to their children, and the hearts of the children to their fathers; or else I will come and strike the land with a curse (Mal. 4:5–6).

People: Children, obey your parents in the Lord, for this is right. "Honor your father and mother"—which is the first commandment with a promise—"that it may go well with you and that you may enjoy long life on the earth" (Eph. 6:1).

Lector: Blessed … are those who hear the word of God and obey it (Luke 11:28).

People: Then [Jesus] went down to Nazareth with them and was obedient to them. … And Jesus grew in wisdom and stature, and in favor with God and men (Luke 2:51, 52).

TABLE CARD INSTRUCTIONS

How to use the table card:

1. Fold the card along the dotted lines to form a triangle. Staple, glue, or tape together.

2. Display for an effective reminder of this week's commandment and Scripture reference.

·· FOLD

We honor and respect authority.

Fourth Commandment

Honor your father and your mother.

·· FOLD

There is no authority except that which God has established.

Rom. 13:1

·· FOLD

THE FIFTH COMMANDMENT

SERMON

God multiply his mercy, his grace, and his peace among us, especially through what he has told us about himself in his Son, our Lord Jesus Christ.

"But who is my *neighbor?*" we ask. We sometimes ask it defensively, sometimes flippantly. If we want to avoid the issue, we ask, "But who is *my* neighbor?"

We know the commandment: "You shall love your neighbor." We have heard it many times. It is the second great commandment of Jesus. God gave it to his Old Testament people on Mount Sinai, Jesus repeated it to the people of his time, and he continues to give it to us through the written Word. But still we ask, "Who is my neighbor?"

We really don't need to ask it any longer; we have no excuse, because the question has long been answered. An expert of the Law tried to test our Lord Jesus by asking, "Who is my neighbor?" Jesus replied with the parable of the Good Samaritan. In essence, Jesus was saying, "You are asking the wrong question. The question is not 'Who is my neighbor?' The question is rather 'Who can I be a neighbor to?' That's the question. The man who fell among the robbers and was left half dead—who was a neighbor to him?"

The expert in the Law was in a bind. The beaten man *was* the neighbor of those who walked by, but the only one who lived out being neighbor, who was the *true* neighbor, was not a neighbor by law. Yet he was the only one who showed mercy. He fixed the bandages on the wounds and paid the hotel bill so that the wounded man could recuperate. The foreigner was the neighbor, because he knew the real question is "Who needs me to be a neighbor?" Now we know, too.

That, my fellow Christians, is what God means when he says in the Fifth Commandment, "You shall not murder" (Ex. 20:13). Rather, because God loves you and your neighbor equally, you shall help and support those who need you.

Now—can you hear the echoes of children crying, children abused, children crushed with words? Can you now see the hurt in the eyes of the young people who have been abandoned by their parents, physically or emotionally? Can you hear the moans of those in wheelchairs or confined to bed at home or in nursing facilities? Can you see people fleeing into the shadowlands because they are of an ethnic minority?

Listen and watch carefully, for oftentimes we are the ones causing the pain. We may be the ones saying the cutting words. We may be the ones who severely punish others. We may be the ones who cause the cringing. We may be the ones who ignore the needy. We may be the ones who say, "Can't somebody else help?"

But Jesus tells us no! It is our responsibility to be neighbors to those who need a neighbor. But it's such a big task! We feel overwhelmed and often fail in our duties as neighbor. Then the words of Jesus convict us and our words begin to fail us. It's at this point that we cannot adequately find a language to express what happens next: With our confession and trust in Jesus, God forgives. We struggle to put it into words, because the compassion of God is totally splendid, is infinitely inclusive, is completely comprehensive, is perfectly all-embracing. You who have abused and hurt and killed one another by your words and your actions, for the sake of Christ Jesus, the Son of God says, "I forgive you."

"Don't kill," God says—and Christ Jesus perfectly fulfilled that commandment for us. Therefore, the heavenly Father can declare you and me to be pardoned for all of those times that we have spoken those wicked words, times that we have expressed hatred within our heart, times we have cut down people with our words. God says we are cleansed because of the perfect obedience of Christ.

What a difference that makes in our lives! When the spirit of Christ lives in our hearts, we are able to pay attention to the letter of the Law and hold back from killing. We are able to hold back from hurting and harming, from taking revenge, from violence, from hurtful language. We are able to work by God's power to live the spirit of the Law. When our enemy hungers we feed him. When she thirsts, we give her drink. We hold back from hurting and harming others. We seek out ways to help. This because we know and have received God's love and forgiveness, and his love for others lives in us.

Obviously, God cares for all individuals as individuals. I believe, however, that we need today to consider two groups of individuals who are particularly vulnerable: those at the beginning and those at the end of life.

No matter what the law of the land says, abortion is murder. That does not mean that we can take it upon ourselves to execute abortionists. Instead, we need to focus our love upon those who have not yet dealt with the guilt of a past abortion or who are contemplating one now—and I include not just women but men also. We need to share with them the strong, powerful love that God has shared through his Son, Jesus—a love that forgives our sins as well as empowers us to live with the responsibility of parenthood, including even when the child might not be "convenient," "perfect," or even "normal" in the eyes of the world.

If you or one of your loved ones is dealing with a past abortion or contemplating one now, please let me know. I'm not about to rant and rave at or expose that person. My goal would be to help her (or him) accept so much of God's forgiving and strengthening love in Jesus that the past will be released and the future God has in mind will be embraced. When we use the power of Christ living in our hearts, we have no trouble saying with St. Paul, "I can do everything through him [Christ] who gives me strength" (Phil. 4:13).

Given the aging of the American population, we also need to concern ourselves with end-of-life issues. And we may properly ask, Where is the balance between the unacceptable extremes of euthanasia and keeping a brain-dead body functioning on a machine? Some guidelines may help as you consider how to handle matters for an aging loved one and/or what directions to leave for others to use at your own life's end.

First, because God alone is Lord of life, he values all life, even those we may think are useless.

Second, God alone knows whether a disease or injury is terminal in a given situation. By itself, pain is not a reason to declare a disease or injury as terminal.

Third, when medical opinion concludes that a person's life will cease in spite of the machines, meaning that God is allowing that human life to cease, life-support systems may be withdrawn. At the same time, the doctor may administer even life-shortening doses of pain killers, because under these conditions, they will not be the cause of death.

In summary:

The commandment in the Hebrew is just two words: Don't murder. But as people forgiven and loved by God in Jesus Christ, we know God is saying a lot more. Hold back from hurting or harming your neighbor, yes—but do stretch forth your hand to help, especially to help the weakest. If that seems difficult, then stretch forth your hand to be reassured that God is helping you.

In the name of the Father, the Son, and the Holy Spirit. Amen.

I Love You, Neighbor

Invocation: In the name of the Father and of the Son and of the Holy Spirit. Amen.

Text: The second is this: "Love your neighbor as yourself." There is no commandment greater than these. Mark 12:31

Insight: The ministry of Jesus Christ shows us that living the Law requires love. It was out of love for the Father and for all people that Jesus went to the cross to offer forgiveness and communion with God. In response, we show our love for God by showing love to our neighbor.

The story of the Good Samaritan shows us that God puts people, even hostile ones, in our path so that we have the opportunity to show love. To do so requires an immersion in the Gospel. The more we are aware of the love and forgiveness given us through Jesus, the better prepared we are to show love and forgiveness to others. Then, when someone does something evil to us, that premeditated love and forgiveness helps us avoid retaliating in a momentary but natural reaction.

The world, though, is very evil. In some places, people are frightened to be alive today. They don't know what others are going to do. If they get in someone's way, they might just as likely be killed as be cursed. There are times when a person comes to the bottom line and things are nonnegotiable. However, St. Paul reminds us that, so far as we are able, we are to live peaceably with others. To do so, we need to turn to the Lord for strength. His perfect love makes up for our imperfect love, and in his love are we given strength.

Prayer: Dear Lord, your Son, Jesus, has taught us how to love others. Yet we live in a world of trouble-makers ...

Not a Keeper, but a Brother

Invocation: In the name of the Father and of the Son and of the Holy Spirit. Amen.

Text: Then the LORD said to Cain, "Where is your brother Abel?" "I don't know," he replied. "Am I my brother's keeper?" Gen. 4:9

Insight: A good number of Christians believe that they do not have to worry about breaking the Fifth Commandment. After all, how many of us will murder someone? Yet Jesus confronts this outward interpretation, warning us that anyone who hates or is angry at another is a murderer and subject to judgement (Matt. 5:22). St. John tells us that whoever loves God will love other people also (1 John 4:19–21).

Tragically, Cain's attitude toward his brother Abel was callous indifference and contempt. The Hebrew word for *keeper* refers to one who watches over animals, not people. Eventually, Cain's attitude led to the killing of his brother.

The Bible describes love and hate not as mere emotions but as attitudes put into action. Consider the account of Jonah. God told him to go to the city of Nineveh to evangelize its people. Jonah's attitude towards the Ninevites was one of hatred and disgust. He was angry at God's compassion for these people whom he considered to be the enemy. Jonah let his attitude result in further disobedience when he tried to flee from God's plan.

What are the Ninevehs in our lives? What attitudes prevent us from sharing God's love and caring for certain people? We too do not deserve the love and mercy that we have received by grace through faith in Jesus. Only out of gratitude to God can we reflect more of God's love in our attitude and actions towards others.

Prayer: Dear Lord, I confess my Ninevehs to you. There are people and groups of people to whom I find it difficult to show love ...

Here's My Cloak, Too

Invocation: In the name of the Father and of the Son and of the Holy Spirit. Amen.

Text: And if someone wants to sue you and take your tunic, let him have your cloak as well. Matt. 5:40

Insight: What happened to the rule of law in public life? In many places, it's alive. But too often people take the law into their own hands in order to be judge, jury, and executioner. Civil justice is perverted into personal vengeance. Personal injury attorneys advertise heavily that they will fight for you to get the largest settlement possible.

In contrast, Jesus speaks of what is expected of us in civil matters. We are to be willing to settle a dispute before it goes to court, and we are to offer even more than the legitimate amount of the claim in order to show no resentfulness to the one who wants to sue us.

How often, though, at work, school, or church do we avoid dialog with people with whom we have a disagreement? Instead of reasoning with them, we first seek retaliation, presenting a case against them to others.

Well-known author Virginia Woolf wrote that people who focus on the wrong things lose their senses. They lose their sense of sight and cannot fairly resolve a dispute. They lose their sense of touch, to take time to touch others with love. They lose their sense of speech and cannot listen to and discuss mutual problems.

Thanks be to God in Christ Jesus, who didn't give us the justice deserved (eternal death), but instead gives us His forgiveness and eternal life. He also gives us the power of the Holy Spirit to show that forgiveness to others.

Prayer: Gracious Father, we, too, have often lost our focus on what your Word expects of us in dealing with others. We too have sought vengeance rather than dialog …

Heaping the Charcoal

Invocation: In the name of the Father and of the Son and of the Holy Spirit. Amen.

Text: If your enemy is hungry, feed him; if he is thirsty, give him something to drink. In doing this, you will heap burning coals on his head. Rom. 12:20

Insight: How do we live a Christian life? In Romans 12, Paul tells us that God calls us to love without hypocrisy, to hate evil, and with humility to defend what is good. We are to exercise active concern for the physical and spiritual needs of others and not return evil, even against those who personally harm us.

Our call is to overpower an enemy with good, leaving vengeance and judgement to God. The phrase "in doing this, you will heap burning coals on his head" likely refers to an ancient ritual. To demonstrate public shame and a spirit of repentance, a person would carry a pan of burning coals on his or head, representing burning shame and guilt. Showing kindness to an evildoer likewise can create a powerful burning shame and a spirit of repentance.

However, to do evil towards someone is our own defeat. Evil toward others begins to destroy the life of Christ in us. Yet Christ's death and resurrection won the victory over our failings. Therefore, by God's grace, through faith in Christ's redemption, we can yet stand perfect before God.

Prayer: Dear Father, it is difficult to be consistent in our love towards all people, in all situations. We admit, at times, to being revengeful …

WORSHIP IDEAS

Hymn Suggestions

"God of Grace and God of Glory"

"Jesu, Jesu, Fill Us with Your Love"

"Make Me a Servant"

"Son of God, Eternal Savior"

Opening Sentences

Pastor: Grace to you and peace from God our Father and the Lord Jesus Christ.

People: Amen.

Pastor: This is the day the LORD has made;

People: Let us rejoice and be glad in it (Ps. 118:24).

Pastor: From the rising of the sun to the place where it sets,

People: The name of the LORD is to be praised (Ps. 113:3).

Pastor: Do not be anxious about anything,

People: But in everything, by prayer and petition, with thanksgiving, present your requests to God (Phil. 4:6).

Confession of Sins

All: O God our Father, we live in a troubled world in which many people need our help. We confess to you that often we claim we do not know where to begin, so we begin nowhere and turn a deaf ear on those who cry for help. We pray for your forgiveness for every time we have ignored a brother or sister we could have helped, but more so for the times we have thought and felt evil toward those who need help. For Jesus' sake give us hearts both cleansed and remade in his image, that we might seek to help in every bodily need. We pray in his name. Amen.

Absolution

Pastor: Our almighty God has cleansed your hearts. He promises you his strength and forgiveness as you live each day and interact with others.

Scripture Readings

Lector: You shall not murder (Ex. 20:13).

People: You have heard that it was said to the people long ago, "Do not murder, … but I tell you that anyone who is angry with his brother will be subject to judgment. Again, anyone who says to his brothers, 'Raca,' is answerable to the Sanhedrin. But anyone who says, 'You fool!' will be in danger of fire of hell" (Matt. 5:21–22).

Lector: You have heard that it was said, "Eye for eye, and tooth for tooth." But I tell you, Do not resist an evil person. If someone strikes you on the right cheek, turn to him the other also. And if someone wants to sue you and take your tunic, let him have your cloak as well. If someone forces you to go one mile, go with him two miles. Give to the one who asks you, and do not turn away from the one who wants to borrow from you (Matt. 5:38–42).

People: Do not repay anyone evil for evil. Be careful to do what is right in the eyes of everybody. If it is possible, as far as it depends on you, live at peace with everyone. Do not take revenge, my friends, but leave room for God's wrath, for it is written: "It is mine to avenge; I will repay," says the Lord. On the contrary: "If your enemy is hungry, feed him; if he is thirsty, give him something to drink. In doing this, you will heap burning coals on his head." Do not be overcome by evil, but overcome evil with good (Rom. 12:17–21).

Call to the Word of God

Pastor: Today, people of God, the Word of the Lord calls us to give attention to our neighbor: not to intrude and not to gossip, but to help and befriend in every bodily need. Let us remind ourselves of the commandment of the Lord, for surely the Lord has much to instruct us.

All: "You shall not murder."

Reflection

Voice 1: Lord, when did we see you hungry and feed you, or thirsty and give you something to drink? When did we see you a stranger and invite you in, or needing clothes and clothe you? When did we see you sick or in prison and go to visit you? (Matt. 25:37–39).

Voice 2: I am homeless. I know I look awful. I haven't had a decent bath or a decent haircut in months. I've been living off of the Rescue Mission and whatever else I scrounge up. I even sell the aluminum cans I pick out of your garbage.

Voice 3: I am mentally retarded. You used to keep me in a special institution. I was safe there, but it was like a prison. Now I live in a group home near you. I wish I had more friends. Would you invite me over for a meal once in a while? I like friends.

Voice 4: I am an illegal alien living up the street from you. I know that I do not have the right to be here, but conditions are so bad in my country that I risked coming here to find work. I need to send some money to my poor family. If all goes well, perhaps I can become a citizen and invite my family to join me. I don't think you like me being here, but perhaps you can try to understand a bit. How can I be a good father if no one lets me provide for my children?

Voice 5: Come, you who are blessed by my Father; take your inheritance, the kingdom prepared for you since the creation of the world. For I was hungry and you gave me something to eat, I was thirsty and you gave me something to drink, I was a stranger and you invited me in, I needed clothes and you clothed me, I was sick and you looked after me, I was in prison and you came to visit me.

TABLE CARD INSTRUCTIONS

How to use the table card:

1. Fold the card along the dotted lines to form a triangle. Staple, glue, or tape together.
2. Display for an effective reminder of this week's commandment and Scripture reference.

.... FOLD

Love your neighbor as yourself.

Fifth Commandment
You shall not murder.

.... FOLD

Be kind and compassionate to one another, forgiving
each other, just as in Christ God forgave you.
Eph. 4:32

.... FOLD

THE SIXTH COMMANDMENT

SERMON

Grace be unto you; mercy and peace in the name of the triune God, the Father and the Son and the Holy Spirit. Amen.

Our text for today is the Sixth Commandment, Ex. 20:14: "You shall not commit adultery."

Because of some misconceptions most of us have had at some point in life, I'm connecting this commandment to one that God gave a lot earlier, when he said, "Have sex." Well … maybe God wasn't that abrupt, but he did say in Gen. 1:28, "Be fruitful," that is, "have children." And the only way that's possible is to have sex. That's why he made two types of bodies and not only one … and why they're attracted to each other.

Whew! What a relief! Sex is okay!

Yes. However … And what a "however" it is!

God established only one relationship in which sex is to happen: marriage.

However …

That limitation of one type of relationship isn't bad; it's good. God points out in Gen. 2:24 that when a man and woman unite through the sexual act, "they will become one flesh." Our romantic songs say that two hearts become one. Well, if they're one and the man commits adultery, he's ripping out his wife's heart. And vice versa. That hurts! God, of course, doesn't want us to be hurt—or to hurt each other. He loves us and wants only the best for us. That's why he said, "You shall not commit adultery."

Marriage: the first institution on earth. Luther commented, "Higher than princedoms and kingships is that of the institution of marriage."

Marriage: so honored by God and so much in danger on account of man! It is honored so by God that when he thinks of the 10 most important things that he wants to talk about and that he wants his people on earth to know, he includes one to protect marriage: "You shall not commit adultery."

Here we have God honoring marriage. Here we have God honoring sex. Here we have God protecting not only marriage as an institution but also the people in it—protecting us by giving us boundaries … so that we can experience the best God has in mind for us, not the worst. Again, that's why out of love God gives boundaries to marriage.

We, however, live in a world in which more and more people seem to think that boundaries are not needed and, in fact, are harmful. We hear people say, "Boundaries stifle my freedom." Or, "Consenting adults should be able to do what ever they want to do, so long they aren't hurting anybody." Or, "Casual sex is harmless; it's normal after all, so no one's going to get hurt by it; it doesn't mean a thing." (If it doesn't mean anything, then why are people disappointed afterward if there's no more social contact?)

Relationships need boundaries, don't they? All social interaction needs boundaries. What happens if there are no boundaries? Everything goes into chaos, that's what happens.

Few matters in life need more boundaries than that of our sexuality. St. Paul gives us the insight of God when he says this: "Flee from sexual immorality. All other sins a man commits are outside his body, but he who sins sexually sins against his own body" (1 Cor. 6:18).

So, there are areas in our life where we need to say no. What are those? Out of love we are to say no to adultery. We do so to protect our marriages as well as the marriages of others that we will not participate in sexual relations with anyone other than our spouse. We are simply committed to saying no, without any excuses. No matter how much someone might come on to us, the Christian answer is no!

And out of love God has set another boundary: there shall be no sexual relations outside of marriage either. That's called fornication. Whether you're a teenager or 20-something or older, God wants to protect you and your possible future marriage.

Now, it doesn't matter if everyone else is doing it. *Everyone* isn't, but it doesn't matter if they were. And it doesn't matter if people try to rationalize it away by saying, "Well, if you love someone and you are committed to someone, you ought to be able to go to bed with that person."

Some people even try to justify themselves by saying, "Well, if we try it out for a little while before we get married then, the marriage will last longer." Not so! It has been proved over and over again that people who live together before marriage have a higher divorce rate than those who remain chaste until married.

Others claim that if they break up as a couple, the pain will be less if they're just having sex and aren't married. The truth is, people who have lived together for any period of time, married or not, go through exactly the same pains and hurts when they break up. Any other claims are pure malarkey.

Sex outside of marriage? The answer is to be no. Not because the pastor says so, but because God says so out of his love and care for you.

Now, out of love God says no to something else. He says we are to say no to divorce. I know—some of you already are divorced. And what's done is done. But that doesn't make divorce right. Neither does it give permission for the future or excuse anyone else.

Listen to what God says through his prophet Malachi (2:13–16):

> You weep and wail because he [God] no longer pays attention to your offerings or accepts them with pleasure from your hands. You ask, "Why?" It is because the LORD is acting as the witness between you and the wife of your youth, because you have broken faith with her, though she is your partner, the wife of your marriage covenant.
>
> Has not the LORD made them one? In flesh and spirit they are his. And why one? Because he was seeking godly offspring. So guard yourself in your spirit, and do not break faith with the wife of your youth.
>
> "I hate divorce," says the LORD God of Israel, "and I hate a man's covering himself with violence as well as with his garment," says the LORD Almighty.
>
> So guard yourself in your spirit, and do not break faith.

Folks, that's just the way the Lord God feels about it.

Now I know that it takes more than one person to create the problems that lead to the death of a marriage. But I also know that there is a solution to those problems when those involved give themselves in obedience to the Lord and forgive one another and live in kindness and in care and in compassion for one another. Love can be rebuilt. Trust can be rebuilt. God can work his best for you. Please don't block his efforts.

Another *no* from God: Out of love, God says we are to say no to same-sex relationships and partnerships. I know it's not socially correct for me to tell you that homosexual and lesbian relationships are contrary to God's will and are sin. But they are. And like any sin they need to be repented of and abandoned.

We are likewise to say no to anything that can dishonor marriage and sex—things such as pornography and sexual harassment. They are warned against in your Bibles. Turn again with me to God's Word, to Ephesians (5:3–4, 11–12):

> But among you there must not be even a hint of sexual immorality, or of any kind of impurity, or of greed, because these are improper for God's holy people. Nor should there be obscenity, foolish talk or coarse joking, which are out of place, but rather thanksgiving.
>
> Have nothing to do with the fruitless deeds of darkness, but rather expose them. For it is shameful even to mention what the disobedient do in secret.

Well, brothers and sisters, what *are* we supposed to do? Is God a big party pooper who only tells us what we're *not* supposed to do? Can Christians have any fun?

Absolutely! God in his love wants us to have great fun, including in sexual matters. And that's why he puts the boundaries on marriage. You can't have fun without boundaries.

Picture a couple of kids out in the park tossing a football back and forth. Then some more guys come along and they decide to have a game. What do they say? "Okay! The line between this tree and that one is the end zone. The sidewalk is the other one. And the side boundaries are between those trees and between those." Even kids know it's ridiculous to think they could plan a game, even if football, without boundaries. You've got to have boundaries to have fun.

And it is in the boundaries of marriage that God said two people can come together in the safety of a commitment to each other and can give themselves to each other because they receive each other as a gift of God. Sex is a holy and precious gift that God has given to you in order that you might be able to become what he wants you to be. These are the boundaries he has stated: "A man will leave his father and mother and be united to his wife, and they will become one flesh" (Gen. 2:24). And he says, "Be fruitful and increase in number; fill the earth and subdue it" (Gen. 1:28).

So God says a big yes to sex, and he puts it in marriage in order to protect us with love and gentleness and care. This is the relationship in which children are to be conceived and nurtured—safe and protected. This is the relationship in which we human beings—you and I—can discover who we really are and in which we can reach the potential that God wants us to reach. In the safety and security and commitment of a dear loved one we can grow and flourish. It's beautiful. That's what can be a most wonderful gift of God.

So—what do we do if we've broken a marriage? If we have violated this commandment? We all have. *All?* Yes! Because Jesus says if you even so much as lust after another person, you have committed adultery in your heart. So—we all have a problem here.

What does God say? He says, "There is forgiveness for you." But now forgiveness is not cheap. It's not just one of these things where we say, "Well, since I'm going to be forgiven anyway, I guess I'll just go out and break this commandment. Isn't it nice that as soon as I've broken it, I can come into church and be forgiven again."

Oh, no. Forgiveness is not cheap. Forgiveness cost the life of the most precious person that ever lived: Jesus himself. But on account of that life for each one of us, repentant Christians receive the complete forgiveness of sins. When we come to him with our minds and hearts laden with guilt over our sins, we can leave those sins at Jesus' feet, and they are buried. God never remembers them again. You will. And your pastor may remind you once in a while in a sermon on the topic so that we can be repentant people. But forgiven sins are not remembered by God.

And then what? Through the Word that God gives us, he also gives strength to go forward as people committed to be honorable in relationships, to be faithful *because God has been faithful to us.*

The cause of our faithfulness is not the law against unfaithfulness. Nor is it because of the possibility of some disease. And if you are a parent, let me tell you: Don't use the threat of AIDS as a way to "force" your children to act like Christians, even though they do need to know the threat of AIDS. We don't use the commandment itself as a call to "be Christian" either! Saying such things to our children (and each other) leads to the erroneous belief that obedience earns salvation. And that's simply not true.

Rather, once we know the grace and the forgiveness of God, his Holy Spirit plants something new in us—the desire to do his will—and we are new creatures. As a result, we *want* to do what pleases God. That's what we say to ourselves and our children. We say no because we love God. God has loved us, and it is out of a heart that loves him in return that we do what pleases and honors God—and he blesses us as well.

So—you and I are the people of God who have been given by God this protection for our sexuality and for our marriages. And this is our commitment to be faithful to our spouses—faithful in the name of the Father and of the Son and of the Holy Spirit. Amen.

I Pledge You My Love

Invocation: In the name of the Father and of the Son and of the Holy Spirit. Amen.

Text: Husbands, love your wives, just as Christ loved the church and gave himself up for her. Eph. 5:25

Insight: "How do I love thee?" When Elizabeth Barrett Browning posed this question she no doubt faced a problem with the English language. We have only one word to describe love. Her solution was to "count the ways."

The Greeks had several words to describe love. Three of these words are used in the New Testament: *eros* for physical love, *phileo* for friendship love, and *agape* for unconditional love. *Agape* love is willing to give, even if it gets nothing in return. It is God's perfect love.

God has set high standards for husbands. In telling men how to love their wives, he did not say to ply her with poetry, candy, and flowers (although these symbols of love should be utilized—often). Rather, God said that men should follow the example of his Son and be willing to give up their life for their wife.

Sometimes, husbands and wives look at each other and see only the child care, cleaning, cooking, yard work, and the rest of the drudgery. As Christians, however, we are able to look at things differently. Jesus' love for the church is our example, and his love for us is what makes it possible for us to love our spouse in the same way.

The next time you ask "How do I love thee" and try to count the ways, count on Jesus to help you love your spouse unconditionally.

Prayer: Christ Jesus, you gave your life for me. Help me to …

I Pledge You Forgiveness

Invocation: In the name of the Father and of the Son and of the Holy Spirit. Amen.

Text: Be kind and compassionate to one another, forgiving each other, just as in Christ God forgave you. Eph. 4:32

Insight: If you're married, you undoubtedly have had at least one argument with your spouse. And if you're not married, be aware that no relationship survives without any disagreement. In a marriage, spouses often blame each other when things fall apart—and have done so since Adam and Eve. But remember: After the fall of Adam and Eve came God's first act of forgiveness.

"Be kind and compassionate," Paul says. But you know that when spouses argue, kindness and compassion fly away. In their place comes Satan to gain a foothold.

Paul's advice is practical as well as theological. When differences of opinion arise, forgiveness is the path to kindness and compassion. Forgiveness is the ultimate act of love. God forgave our sins by sending his only Son to die on the cross. Strengthened in his love and forgiveness, we too are able to forgive and be renewed in love.

Prayer: Dear God, so fill me with your love that I automatically forgive others as you have forgiven me. Especially …

I Pledge You Help

Invocation: In the name of the Father and of the Son and of the Holy Spirit. Amen.

Text: The LORD God said, "It is not good for the man to be alone. I will make a helper suitable for him." Gen. 2:18

Insight: Start at the beginning: Why did God make man and a woman? Why did God's divine design bring a man and a woman together in marriage and begin the miracle of one-ness?

Our text introduces the concept of a helper. Where there are two, there is twice the strength. If one begins to fall, the other can steady him. If one starts to slip, the other can catch her. We can help each other not only with menial tasks around the home, but also with our spiritual walk with God. In the words of King Solomon, "Two are better than one" (Eccl. 4:9).

But even two are not enough. We must rely on the power of the Holy Spirit to help us help each other. When husband and wife pledge their faithfulness in mind, body, and spirit, God's divine design is fulfilled. God enters the union, and then there are three. And, as Eccl. 4:12 says, "A cord of three strands is not quickly broken."

Prayer: Help us, Holy Spirit, to uphold one another in all we say and do. Particularly ...

I Pledge You My Body

Invocation: In the name of the Father and of the Son and of the Holy Spirit. Amen.

Text: Has not the LORD made them one? In flesh and spirit they are his. And why one? Because he was seeking godly off-spring. So guard yourself in your spirit, and do not break faith with the wife of your youth. Mal. 2:15

Insight: What do you do when faced with a devotion about the Sixth Commandment? Adultery, sex, and immorality are top-ics that, frankly, make Christians a little uncomfortable. We don't like to talk about them. But God does. He gave us the gift of sex. God is pleased when a man and a woman marry and use this gift to build a Christian home and family.

Unfortunately, society actively rebels against God's plan to keep sexual desires within marriage. Our own free will is constantly bombarded with sexual invitations—invitations we Christians want to reject. This is no easy task, for Satan preys on our weaknesses and tempts us to remove sexual desire out of the confines set by God. And in so doing, Satan's twisted logic leads us to think of sex as evil and dirty.

Sex, however, is *not* evil or dirty—it is God-made. When a Christian man and woman become one, God's perfect love grows in them through his Word and Spirit. In a Christian home, father and mother deeply love each other. The parents and the children find real joy, for Christ keeps his promise to be present, to love, forgive, and to bless.

Prayer: Create in me a clean heart, O God, and ...

WORSHIP IDEAS

Hymn Suggestions

"Take My Life, O Lord, Renew"

"Great Is Thy Faithfulness"

"We Are One in the Bond of Love"

"May We Your Precepts, Lord, Fulfill"

"Renew Me, O Eternal Light"

"How I Love You"

Opening Sentence

Pastor: Our God is faithful. He is faithful in all his ways. He is faithful in love and mercy, in kindness and loyalty. He is faithful in forgiveness.

People: "Your love, O LORD, reaches to the heavens, your faithfulness to the skies" (Ps. 36:5).

Pastor: God is faithful. In him "love and faithfulness meet together, righteousness and peace kiss each other" (Ps. 85:10).

People: "I will sing of the LORD's great love forever; with my mouth I will make your faithfulness known through all generations" (Ps. 89:1).

Confession of Sins

Pastor: Confident of his faithfulness, especially in his love and forgiveness, we confess our unfaithfulness, our failures in love, and our failures in commitments.

All: Faithful Father, because you have said that you will never take your love from us and that you will never betray your faithfulness, we admit that time and again we have failed you. We have been unfaithful in thought, word, and deed. Though we commit ourselves to you and to one another, we do not keep these commitments. We acknowledge we are full of sin from birth and need your mercy. Forgive us for Jesus' sake. In your faithfulness restore us to you and to our relationships with one another. In Jesus' holy name we pray.

Absolution

Pastor: Hear the Word of the Lord: "Because of the LORD's great love we are not consumed, for his compassions never fail. They are new every morning; great is your faithfulness ... The LORD is good to those whose hope is in him, to the one who seeks him; it is good to wait quietly for the salvation of the LORD" (Lam. 3:22–23, 25–26). Salvation is yours. God gives it to you on account of his Son, Jesus our Lord. Continue in his peace and forgiveness.

People: We will. Amen!

Scripture Readings

Lector: At the beginning of creation God "made them male and female." "For this reason a man will leave his father and mother and be united to his wife, and the two will become one flesh." So they are no longer two, but one. Therefore what God has joined together, let man not separate (Mark 10:6–9).

People: Marriage should be honored by all, and the marriage bed kept pure, for God will judge the adulterer and all the sexually immoral (Heb. 13:4).

Lector: The grace of God that brings salvation has appeared to all men. It teaches us to say "No" to ungodliness and worldly passions, and to live self-controlled, upright and godly lives in this present age (Titus 2:11–12).

People: Finally, brothers, whatever is true, whatever is noble, whatever is right, whatever is pure, whatever is lovely, whatever is admirable—if anything is excellent or praiseworthy—think about such things (Phil. 4:8).

The Word of the Lord and the Cries of His People

Pastor: The Word of the Lord: You shall not commit adultery.

The Cry of Youth: Hear me, O Lord. I am young. Before me lie the many temptations of sex. Already I know the pull of that drive; I have felt the longing of my heart for another. But I am so confused. All around me I am invited to do whatever feels good to me. Sex is peddled before my eyes every day in countless ways. I am told I cannot grow up without having sex with someone—and the sooner the better. I am told just to make sure it is safe sex. Is that what you want, God? Help me to be faithful to you.

The Cry of the Wedding Day: It is my wedding day, the happiest day of my life! We will always be in love. Or will we? Will our marriage go the way my parents' did? Will we stick it out only until the going gets rough? Will we soon fight, forget to say "I'm sorry," and hold in grudges and resentment? Will we lose sight of each other? Will I be satisfied with my spouse *all* the days of my life? How can we learn what it takes to keep our marriage together, our lives happy? Help us, Lord. Help us to be wise and not to listen to those whose hearts are not right with you. Help us make our marriage work.

The Cry of Divorce: Hear me, O Lord. I am broken and full of shame. My spouse left me for someone else. Once I was the apple of my partner's eye. But as the years have gone by we have drifted apart and now my spouse has found someone new to talk to and to share innermost thoughts, secrets, and desires. Part of it is my fault. I have given myself so fully to other things and have neglected my spouse. But I did not know things had reached this point of looking elsewhere for affection. I am crushed, broken and alone. I need your help; I need healing. What can I do? Help me, Lord.

Pastor: The Word of the Lord: For this reason I kneel before the Father, from whom his whole family in heaven and on earth derives its name. I pray that out of his glorious riches he may strengthen you with power through his Spirit in your inner being, so that Christ may dwell in your hearts through faith. And I pray that you, being rooted and established in love, may have power, together with all the saints, to grasp how wide and long and high and deep is the love of Christ, and to know this love that surpasses knowledge—that you may be filled to the measure of all the fullness of God (Eph. 3:14–19).

Be imitators of God, therefore, as dearly loved children and live a life of love, just as Christ loved us and gave himself up for us as a fragrant offering and sacrifice to God (Eph. 5:1–2).

TABLE CARD INSTRUCTIONS

How to use the table card:

1. Fold the card along the dotted lines to form a triangle. Staple, glue, or tape together.

2. Display for an effective reminder of this week's commandment and Scripture reference.

.... FOLD

Marriage—so honored by God!

Sixth Commandment
You shall not commit adultery.

.... FOLD

Whatever is true, whatever is noble, whatever is right,

whatever is pure, whatever is lovely, whatever is admirable

—if anything is excellent or praiseworthy—

think about such things.

Phil. 4:8

.... FOLD

THE SEVENTH COMMANDMENT

SERMON

O Lord, may the words of our mouths and the meditations of our hearts be pleasing to you, our Rock and our Redeemer. Amen.

We look today at the Seventh Commandment, "You shall not steal." We do so, though, in the context of another word from God, Ps. 24:1: "The earth is the LORD's, and everything in it, the world, and all who live in it."

"The earth is the LORD's"? That almost sounds like saying, What is mine is not mine and what is yours is not yours. That doesn't sound American. Maybe that's communist. No, the communist says, what is mine is the government's, what is yours is the government's, and what is my neighbor's is the government's, too. So maybe it's socialism. No, socialism says, what is mine is my neighbor's, what is yours is my neighbor's, and what's my neighbor's is mine *and* yours.

So it's not communism, it's not socialism, and it's certainly not capitalism. What is it? It's biblical. It says, what's mine is God's, what's yours is God's, and what is my neighbor's is God's, too. Yet, even though it's his, all of it, he sees fit to entrust us with the management of it. Don't steal, because the property belongs to God. And there's more! Because your neighbor's stuff actually belongs to God, you need to help your neighbor take care of it for God.

I know. It's bad enough that you have to protect the goods in your charge, much less turn around and protect the goods in your neighbor's. But that's the way it is. One man was reminded of that when he was traveling with his son and they stopped for some fast food. He paid for it with a 10, but they gave him change for a 20. As he sat eating, he looked at the extra 10 dollars and thought, "Yeah, finally I'm getting back what's been taken from me by so many people so often." So he put it in his pocket, and the two went to the car.

He had only driven a block, when his conscience got the better of him. He turned around and returned the 10 dollars. Even though he didn't get a thank you from the cashier, he experienced the joy of protecting someone else's goods (and of setting a standard for his son). For you see, as Christians, we pledge, "I will protect what is yours, my neighbor."

There are four losses in thievery. First, the person stealing loses reputation and ultimately a relationship with God. Second, since all is God's, God loses, too. Third, the person stolen from has lost property. And fourth—and this is one we don't think about often—since God has entrusted my neighbor with the care of property, if I rip him off, I am stealing his opportunity to manage for God the things entrusted to him.

Under the Seventh Commandment, God calls me to protect what is yours, my neighbor.

What does that mean for those of you who are employees? It means that you faithfully serve the company, that you will both not steal and will give an honest day's labor for an honest day's wage. That's what it means.

If you're an employer, it means that those who work for you will be treated honestly and with integrity; that they will be seen and accepted as fellow servants of God, not one better than another; and it means that you will ensure that the place in which they work is safe, physically and emotionally. That's what it means.

The commandment touches also my duty to community, state, and nation. I keep my front yard looking beautiful for the sake of the community. And when it comes time to pay my taxes, I pay what is due for the sake of the common good.

Oh, how I wish I could say there isn't a Christian who violates any of those principles! The truth is, this principle is violated all the time. Over 460 years ago Martin Luther wrote in his Large Catechism,

> At the market and in everyday business the same fraud prevails in full force. One person openly cheats another with defective merchandise, false measures, dishonest weights, and bad coins, and take advantage of him by underhanded tricks and sharp practices and crafty dealing. Or again, one swindles another in a trade and deliberately fleeces, skins, and torments him. Who can even describe or imagine it all? In short, thievery is the most common craft and the largest guild on earth. If we look at mankind in all its conditions, it is nothing but a vast, wide stable full of great thieves.

> These men are called gentlemen swindlers or big operators. Far from being picklocks and sneak-thieves who loot a cash box, they sit in office chairs and are called great lords and honorable, good citizens, and yet with a great show of legality they rob and steal (LC I 227–29).

Why, that could be a quote from *Time* or *Newsweek!* That's our society. As I said, I wish that none of us were guilty of any of those things. But who of us always deals totally honestly with everybody in every circumstance? And so we find ourselves condemned by God's Law. Especially disconcerting is the fact that when we say "I will protect what is yours," the "yours" refers to God's stuff, his property, everything. "The earth is the LORD's, and everything in it, the world, and all who live in it."

Because everything is the Lord's, the Seventh Commandment affects one more area of life: stealing from God. Listen to what he says through the prophet Malachi, chapter 3, verses 8–10:

"Will a man rob God? Yet you rob me.

"But you ask, 'How do we rob you?'

"In tithes and offerings. You are under a curse—the whole nation of you—because you are robbing me. Bring the whole tithe into the storehouse, that there may be food in my house. Test me in this," says the LORD Almighty, "and see if I will not throw open the floodgates of heaven and pour out so much blessing that you will not have room enough for it."

Wow!

Do you see now the picture of stewardship inherent in the Seventh Commandment? Picture a rich man who owns two farms side by side: the one you manage and the one I manage. If I steal crops from the farm you manage, I'm really stealing not from you but from the rich man. The same holds true if you steal from the farm on which I'm living. And it's just as bad—if not worse—when either one of us or both of us refuse to pay the rich man his tenth of the profits at the end of the season. Talk about brazen stealing! Most people share-cropping today have to pay 50 percent. Our rich man asks for only 10 percent—and usually doesn't receive it.

Obviously, the rich man in my little parable is God. But God does more than simply provide us the land to farm: he also gives us the seed to plant, the fertilizer and water to make it grow, he even stakes us while we wait for the harvest.

That's why he can say as he did in Malachi, "Test me. As a way to acknowledge that all this is mine," God says, "return a tenth to me—and then watch how I bless you! See if I will not throw open the floodgates of heaven and pour out so much blessing that you will not have room enough for it."

I wish I could say that Christians are good in their stewardship. But the usual statistic is that 20 percent of the people in any organization give 80 percent of the money. The other 20 percent of the funds are given by about 50 percent of the people. And about 30 percent usually give nothing.

To say this from the pulpit can be a little dangerous. I heard about one preacher who sent to his members a stewardship letter that referred to God's ownership. The letter listed what a thank-you tithe to the Lord would mean in terms of dollar amounts. When that pastor visited one of the members who was upset by the letter, the parishioner asked him, "Did you send this out to me?"

When the pastor affirmed that he had, the man said, "Then you better get the [blank] out of here before I kill you." He got up, chased the pastor out of the house, and headed for his pickup and a rifle. Fortunately, by the time he unlocked the truck, the pastor had hightailed it out of sight.

Dangerous or not, God's ownership of everything must be proclaimed. I'm not scared, though; I'm sad—sad because the way we handle the goods of this world reflect how we think of and about God. It makes me sad also because most of us are not experiencing all the blessing that God wants to give to our life. What did he say? "Test me in this … and see if I will not throw open the floodgates of heaven and pour out so much blessing that you will not have room enough for it." He wants to give you more blessings then you know how to cope with.

I know that some of you have a tough time when it comes to hearing the word *stewardship*. Some of you are new to the faith. To others it simply looks impossible. Still others don't control the purse strings in the family. I understand that.

But now let's get some things straight. God never asks for anything he doesn't first give. Never, ever. He is somewhat like the father who around Christmas slips his 10-year-old son a $20 bill so that the son can go out and buy him a Christmas present and then doesn't even ask for the change. That's God. He first gives. And then he asks you to give back out of what you have received. So if you don't have, you can't give. That's no problem. But you can give of what he has given to you.

Allow me to take you back to my parable about living on the farm of the rich man. Actually, everyone in the world is living on one of his farms. Look again at what he has done and is doing for you and yours. Savor in your mind all the fine cuisine you have eaten for all these years. Touch the clothes you wear to ensure yourself that you are not naked. For just a moment, close your eyes to picture all the friends and loved ones who have filled your life. Open your eyes to see where you are now: in church.

Millions upon millions of people around the world have received the same physical blessings that you have—some more, some less. But you have been blessed with knowing *who* has given you these things—*and why*. "God so loved the world that he gave …" not only the things of this earth but "his one and only Son, that whoever believes in him shall not perish but have eternal life" (John 3:16).

You and I both know how we would react if we were the rich man and our tenants withheld our share of the profits. That's why it is utterly important for us to understand that our unfaithfulness does not change God's faithfulness to us. When he talks about opening the storehouse and pouring it out, he is *not* saying the converse, that he will withhold his love and forgiveness from us just because we haven't been good stewards.

I stand before you to tell you if you never gave a nickel to the Lord's work, never, he would not withhold his forgiveness, life, and salvation. When he sent his son, Jesus, he did so to pay for the guilt of every sin, every last one, to bury them, never to be reminded of them again. And having done that, he also sent his Spirit into your heart so that you might know and believe that all this in fact was done for *you*.

Look inside your own heart. Is life on the rich man's farm really a drag? Or are you grateful to live here—and especially grateful to know who he is and what his Son has done for you? I believe that the reason you are here this morning is your gratefulness, that you love being loved by God and love the new life he is working in you. I also know that we Christians are simultaneously saint and sinner—which means that living the Seventh Commandment (as well as any other commandment) is a day-to-day struggle. But, I know too that God is with us in that struggle, that he empowers us to *be* the people he has recreated us to be, that all things are possible with him.

He creates in our hearts the desire to have a heart that beats like his heart and that is like him in being generous. The greatest joy in life is to reflect our father. And in so doing, then we protect and we are protected. I protect what is yours, and you protect what is mine. And together we protect what is God's for the stewardship of his church.

And what's the result? The Gospel is proclaimed and the forgiveness that is freely given is offered to all.

In the name of the Father and of the Son and of the Holy Spirit. Amen.

Stewards of Spiritual Matters

Invocation: In the name of the Father and of the Son and of the Holy Spirit. Amen.

Text: Do not store up for yourselves treasures on earth, where moth and rust destroy, and where thieves break in and steal. But store up for yourselves treasures in heaven, where moth and rust do not destroy, and where thieves do not break in and steal. For where your treasure is, there your heart will be also. Matt. 6:19–21

Insight: If you want to see a manifestation of the first part of the verse, just look inside most garages or basements. Moth and rust certainly do destroy! Years of accumulation easily prove that. And when you see once-prized possessions turned to junk, you wonder how you could have even once allowed the stuff of life to replace the Staff of Life: Jesus, our Lord and Savior. "Seek first his kingdom and his righteousness, and all these things [food and clothing] will be given to you as well" (Matt. 6:33).

As God's stewards of spiritual matters, we are concerned about the same things that are of concern to him. Whether it's our growing relationship with him or our concern for others, we are involved with his kingdom, thankful for his rule in our hearts as we spread the Good News of his rule to the hearts of others.

It has always amazed me that the Lord elects to work through us to accomplish his will. We have all been recruited. There is no sideline for spectators. He has redeemed us to be his own. He has forgiven us so that he might have our hearts. How grateful we are that as citizens of heaven, our spiritual eyes can see what God is doing through us and in us as he prepares us for our eternal treasures.

Prayer: Lord, I ask that you give me a clearer understanding of my heavenly citizenship. Give me a growing concern for spiritual matters. I pray for …

Stewards of What Is Given to Us

Invocation: In the name of the Father and of the Son and of the Holy Spirit. Amen.

Text: For everyone who has will be given more, and he will have an abundance. Whoever does not have, even what he has will be taken from him. Matt. 25:29

Insight: When Jesus taught, he often went behind the printed word to the spirit God intended. Here are two illustrations of this from the Sermon on the Mount, Matthew 5:

1. You have heard that it was said, "Eye for eye, and tooth for tooth." But I tell you, Do not resist an evil person. If someone strikes you on the right cheek, turn to him the other also (vv. 38–39).

2. You have heard that it was said, "Love your neighbor and hate your enemy." But I tell you: Love your enemies and pray for those who persecute you (vv. 43–44).

Jesus might also have said of the Seventh Commandment, "You have heard it was said, 'You shall not steal.' But I tell you, be faithful stewards of the gifts given to you."

When I find that I'm not responding to the parable of the talents in Matthew 25 as I should I try to stop and remind myself of these points:

1. Don't focus on yourself. Servants serve the Master and should not be too concerned with themselves.

2. Don't focus on the gifts. Confusion arises when I feel I have little to give.

3. Don't focus on the results. The only steward with no results was the one that was concerned about results.

4. Do focus on the abundance of his love and forgiveness. It is so great that it leads us to abundance sharing.

5. Look forward to our final affirmation from the Lord: "Well done, good and faithful servant! … Come and share your master's happiness!" (Matt. 25:21).

Prayer: Lord, help me to see more clearly that my life is a gift to be shared. Help me to be a good steward as I …

Stewardship of What Is Our Neighbor's

Invocation: In the name of the Father and of the Son and of the Holy Spirit. Amen.

Text: Each of you should look not only to your own interests, but also to the interests of others. Phil. 2:4

Insight: I've got a confession to make. When I hear that one of my business competitors is not doing well, a part of me says, "Yes!" rather than "Oh, no!" I'm also a bit jealous when someone else does better than I. Someone wins and someone loses; it's called the competitive spirit. Yet I know that neither of these feelings is right; they both need to be examined in the light of God's Word.

Philippians 2:4 tells us to look to the interests of others as well as our own. We are to help our neighbors to improve and protect their property and business. We even are to rejoice when we see them prosper. At the same time, we have the God-given responsibility to care for ourselves and our families. The problem is in balancing our own needs with those of others.

Philippians 2:1 gives us the answer: Be united with Christ and his love. In union with him and in fellowship with the Spirit, we have the tenderness and compassion to follow the example of Jesus. He emptied himself of his divine rights and took on the form of a servant, a servant concerned only with doing the will of his Father. Because of his servant work, you and I, as forgiven and restored people, also are able to be servants to those who need us as well as to our competitors, our neighbors.

As a steward of what is my neighbor's, my *attitude* is as important as what I *do*. When I follow Jesus' example of a servant, I naturally am concerned for others. My own needs become less important, and I am assured that God is working through me for his good purposes.

Prayer: Lord, I may not have more time but I pray that you would give me a greater compassion for the needs of others. Help me to see opportunities to use my gifts for others. Especially I pray for ...

Stewards of Those Who Have Little

Invocation: In the name of the Father and of the Son and of the Holy Spirit. Amen.

Text: He who has been stealing must steal no longer, but must work, doing something useful with his own hands, that he may have something to share with those in need. Eph. 4:28

Insight: I can remember a time as a young parent when I could not find a job and we really had only one or two day's supply of groceries. As the Lord often does, a generous gift came at the last minute that gave me a tremendous boost. I offered to pay back the money when I was able. The giver simply said, "No, just pass it on to someone else in need when you can."

If you've had a similar circumstance, you know the many emotions tied to it. It's normally met with the reaction "I wouldn't trade that experience for a million dollars, but I won't give you a nickel to go through it again."

On the million dollar side, the experience left me with a sense of responsibility to pass on the gift I received to others. However, because of our current welfare system, getting personally involved with the needs of others doesn't seem to be necessary anymore. It is so easy now for me to assume that the government—or at least someone with greater resources than I have—will help.

As I reread Eph. 4:28, I am reminded that one of the most important reasons for working is not to acquire possessions or attain financial security, but rather to look to the needs of others and willingly share what I have with others. We each have a gift to pass on. As has been said often, the world has ample resources for everyone. It's just that the distribution system does not work well.

God, however, distributes his love lavishly—to all in need. It is on account of that love that we too can share with those in need. Together we are the body of Christ to those in need.

Prayer: Father in heaven, as you have given so freely to me, help me not to hold on to my gifts but to share with others in need. Help me to respond by ...

WORSHIP IDEAS

Hymn Suggestions

"Here Is the Tenfold Sure Command"

"Oh, that the Lord Would Guide My Ways"

"Lord, Be Glorified"

"Turn Your Eyes upon Jesus"

"I Love You, Lord"

Opening Sentences

Pastor: The earth is the LORD's, and everything in it,

People: The world, and all who live in it (Ps. 24:1).

Pastor: "The silver is mine and the gold is mine," declares the LORD Almighty (Hag. 2:8),

People: And the cattle on a thousand hills (Ps. 50:10).

Pastor: Therefore you are to protect what is the Lord's

People: And guard that which he has given to others.

Pastor: In the name of him to whom all belongs,

People: The Father, the Son, and the Holy Spirit. Amen.

Confession of Sins

People: Lord, we recognize that you are the owner of all, and that you give of what is yours and entrust it to each one according to your will. We acknowledge that we sin daily as we mismanage what has been entrusted to us, and as we fail to help our neighbor keep all that is his. Forgive us for this our sin, and restore us in your mercy. Give us hearts that desire to be honest in all our dealings that we may reflect the integrity of your heart. In Jesus' name we pray it.

Absolution

Pastor: As a called and ordained servant of the Word, I proclaim to you the forgiveness of all of your sins. By the blood of Jesus Christ you are cleansed. The Lord Almighty gives you the power to live as his sons and daughters, reflecting him in all your external dealings with your neighbor. Amen.

Scripture Readings

Lector: Do not use dishonest standards when measuring length, weight or quantity (Lev. 19:35).

People: The wicked borrow and do not repay, but the righteous give generously (Ps. 37:21).

Lector: He who has been stealing must steal no longer, but must work, doing something useful with his own hands, that he may have something to share with those in need (Eph. 4:28).

People: Each of you should look not only to your own interests, but also to the interests of others (Phil. 2:4).

Lector: Give to one who asks you, and do not turn away from the one who wants to borrow from you (Matt. 5:42).

People: Do not forget to do good and to share with others, for with such sacrifices God is pleased (Heb. 13:16).

TABLE CARD INSTRUCTIONS

How to use the table card:

1. Fold the card along the dotted lines to form a triangle. Staple, glue, or tape together.
2. Display for an effective reminder of this week's commandment and Scripture reference.

FOLD

You shall not steal.

The Seventh Commandment

We will protect all that is yours.

FOLD

Share with others, for with such sacrifices

God is pleased.

Heb. 13:16

FOLD

THE EIGHTH COMMANDMENT

SERMON

In the precious name of Jesus, my brothers and sisters. Amen.

The Eighth Commandment: You shall not give false testimony against your neighbor.

Oh, the tongue—whatever shall we do with it? It's only a little part of our body, but it has such potential to destroy. The tongue. Like the mouse on a computer or a joy stick on a helicopter, the little thing controls the whole hardware. The tongue: with it we bless God, and with it we curse people whom God has made.

Listen to the way the apostle James worded it:

> If anyone is never at fault in what he says, he is a perfect man, able to keep his whole body in check.
>
> When we put bits into the mouths of horses to make them obey us, we can turn the whole animal. Or take ships as an example. Although they are so large and are driven by strong winds, they are steered by a very small rudder wherever the pilot wants to go. Likewise the tongue is a small part of the body, but it makes great boasts. Consider what a great forest is set on fire by a small spark. The tongue also is a fire, a world of evil among the parts of the body. It corrupts the whole person, sets the whole course of his life on fire, and is itself set on fire by hell.
>
> All kinds of animals, birds, reptiles and creatures of the sea are being tamed and have been tamed by man, but no man can tame the tongue. It is a restless evil, full of deadly poison.
>
> With the tongue we praise our Lord and Father, and with it we curse men, who have been made in God's likeness. Out of the same mouth come praise and cursing. My brothers, this should not be. Can both fresh water and salt water flow from the same spring? My brothers, can a fig tree bear olives, or a grapevine bear figs? Neither can a salt spring produce fresh water (James 3:2–12).

Oh, if we could just check the tongue with a bit! If we could just control it as well as one person does a big ship with just a tiny little rudder! But we don't. And one slip of the tongue works like a little spark that ignites a great forest fire. We can say things that can cause people to hurt a long time. Some people never recover. It's a deadly thing, this tongue.

Remember the story in the Old Testament of King Ahab and Naboth? Ahab wanted a vineyard close to his own palace, so that he could plant there a vegetable garden. Naboth owned it, but could not sell it because it was part of the family inheritance. So King Ahab pouted. Queen Jezebel saw Ahab and said, "Oh, the king shouldn't have to pout; he should have his way"—and she proceeded to send letters to the courts and the elders of the city accusing Naboth of cursing God and the king. Then she hired two false witnesses to testify to that in court. The result was that Naboth was condemned and hung—and Ahab got his vegetable garden.

False witnesses ... the tongue ... the ability to kill. It still has that power, doesn't it?

God says, "You shall not give false testimony against your neighbor." That's the command of God. Why is it, brothers and sisters, that it's so hard to keep? Why is it that we get such pleasure when we speak negatively about someone else?

Jesus gave the answer: we have a problem with our heart.

> The things that come out of the mouth come from the heart, and these make a man "unclean." For out of the heart come evil thoughts, murder, adultery, sexual immorality, theft, false testimony, slander. These are what make a man "unclean" (Matt. 15:18–20).

What comes from the heart and then out of the mouth? Lots of evil—including false testimony and slander. The problem is our heart.

Oh, I know we have a tendency to say, "I'm not really to blame for that, because, after all, it's just a natural thing, you know."

We *like* to blame God, don't we? As one poster says, "If God did not want me to judge and condemn others, why did he make me so good at it?" That's what we *like* to do: blame God. But it doesn't work. The fact is, we *choose* to think, speak, and do evil. James says in his letter,

> When tempted, no one should say, "God is tempting me." For God cannot be tempted by evil, nor does he tempt anyone; but each one is tempted when, by his own evil desire, he is dragged away and enticed. Then, after desire has conceived, it gives birth to sin; and sin, when it is full-grown, gives birth to death (1:13–15).

The fact is, we have chosen to do evil ever since our birth. Psalm 51:5 says, "I was sinful at birth, sinful from the time my mother conceived me." Therefore we plead in that same psalm, "Create in me a pure heart, O God, and renew a steadfast spirit within me" (v. 10).

A new heart—that's what we need. Angioplasty or a by-pass operation or other repair work won't do. We need a new heart, one that is attuned to God, one that is pliable to God, one that's responsive to his will. "Restore to me the joy of your salvation and grant me a willing spirit, to sustain me," says verse 12. That's what we need: that the Holy Spirit give us a new heart that has a willingness to it—a willingness, an openness toward God.

The Good News for you and for me is that God *has* given us our new heart in our Baptism. Do not think for even a moment that when the water touched you, the event was just some kind of symbolic act or a way for you to offer yourself to God. No! Baptism is the most powerful moment that can ever happen to a person on this planet. It is when God, connecting his Word and his promise with that water, says, "I am going to give *myself* to you."

With Christ living in us, we now are able to see clearly something we previously saw only dimly if at all: Every human being has been created by God and in his likeness. As such, every human being—including those who have not believed in Christ and are, therefore, not saved—every human being is touched with God-given dignity. That's why the apostle James is surprised when believers use the same tongue that praises God to also curse God's likeness: "With the tongue we praise our Lord and Father, and with it we curse men, who have been made in God's likeness" (3:9).

Part of our problem in sin is that we conclude that only in comparison to others can we see ourselves as valuable. Fill in the blank: "I'm _____ and you're not, so I'm better than you." Sometimes we word it in the reverse: "You're bad for being _____, and I'm not; so I'm better than you." You know better than I how you fill in those blanks. "I'm white, black, a college grad, a union member, a woman, a man, a heterosexual, a democrat, a republican; you should know also that I am not a crook, a pedophile, a tightwad, an over-indulgent parent, or an all-around scoundrel. Therefore, I'm better than you are."

At the end of the sixth day of creation, the day on which he created Adam and Eve, God looked at all he had made and "it was very good" (Gen. 1:31). Then sin cost us perfection. Apart from his Son, God looks at people and says, "There is not a righteous man on earth who does what is right and never sins" (Eccl. 7:20). "All have sinned and fall short of the glory of God" (Rom. 3:23). But through his Son, God still looks at people and reaffirms through James that we are made in his likeness (3:9).

Because we are baptized, because God has created a new heart within us, we can look at ourselves first and see our true dignity. I am worth something in spite of my sinful nature and my many individual sins. I am worth something in spite of my unwillingness to take perfect care of this body. I am worth something in spite of my opinion that my body is not as good as someone else's.

I am worth something because I am human and the crown of God's creation. We humans are like Stradivariuses in an orchestra of kazoos— there is no comparison between us and the rest of creation.

And that's not all! God not only created us humans, he loves us. He loves us so much "that he gave his one and only Son, that whoever believes in him shall not perish but have eternal life" (John 3:16). And even better than that: We who have been baptized know this to be true.

Therefore, since God created "little ol' me" and loved me this much, how could I ever disparage myself? How could I ever berate myself for my past and now forgiven sins? How could I ever claim that God made some mistake when he made me? No—God has created me and has redeemed me, and therefore I will never again speak ill of myself.

It should come as no surprise that I do not want ever to speak ill of any other human either. Because I am still human, I know that I cannot live the perfect life, but as a Christian I still want to. And as a Christian my eyes have been opened to see that I'm not the only human created and loved by God; so are you! How fantastic! We're the same—neither one better or worse than the other, but both created and loved by God! Wow!

Now it's no longer just God who speaks the Eighth Commandment, but I say it of myself: I do not want to give false testimony against you or slander you or speak ill of you. In Christ, my love "always protects, always trusts, always hopes, always perseveres" (1 Cor. 13:7). And when you are less than perfect even as I am less than perfect, "love covers over a multitude of sins" (1 Peter 4:8).

We will not ever keep this commandment perfectly. It is impossible for us to do so. But what we can do day after day is return to our Baptism. That's more than just an intellectual phrase; it is that whole process of remembering who and what we are—the created and forgiven people of God, people who have been given new hearts, hearts filled with the Holy Spirit. Returning to our Baptism also means that God is opening our eyes to see what he sees in each of us: his beloved crown of creation. And that's true witness!

In the name of the Father and of the Son and of the Holy Spirit. Amen.

Speaking Truthfully

Invocation: In the name of the Father and of the Son and of the Holy Spirit. Amen.

Text: Each of you must put off falsehood and speak truthfully to his neighbor, for we are all members of one body. Eph. 4:25

Insight: One Friday evening, as I was sitting on the couch, relaxing after a long week of work, the phone rang. As my daughter dove for the phone, I told her that if it was for me, she should say I wasn't home. I admit, I definitely did not set a good example of our text, of speaking truthfully!

I remember many years ago when a school friend and I had an argument. She made a comment to me that was untrue and very hurtful—and then went on to tell my other friends. This incident blew over after only a few days, but still, after all these years, I feel the sting of that comment, even though it was untrue. Those bad feelings still come back to the surface now and then.

God's will for us is that we experience the abundant life— a life of joy, peace, and harmony. Being human, we don't always trust God to create such a life for us—and therefore we try to create it for ourselves out of lies, half-truths, and innuendos. We forget that a necessary ingredient in God's recipe for this abundant life is honest and truthful communication and dealings with others at home, at work, at church —everywhere. Because of Jesus Christ, we are able to so live. After all, now that we know God has loved us and forgiven us because of Jesus, we also can see that he has worked every good for us. We trust his decisions for our good and, therefore, know of no reason to try to get anything else by lies or deceit. Since we have everything good, what else is there we want? Nothing. Therefore, we are able to go forward in the joy, peace, and harmony of the abundant life by the grace of our Savior and speak the truth.

Prayer: Lord, thank you for your forgiveness. Help me to speak the truth in love and to build up those around me. Help me especially with …

Withholding Judgment

Invocation: In the name of the Father and of the Son and of the Holy Spirit. Amen.

Text: Do not judge, and you will not be judged. Do not condemn, and you will not be condemned. Forgive, and you will be forgiven. Luke 6:37

Insight: A couple of summers ago, my five-year-old daughter and I went on an outing to the beach. While we were lounging in the sun, we noticed a very suspicious-looking character, so we decided to keep our eye on him. Sure enough, after about 20 minutes, he moved himself right next to someone else's beach towel, started to go through a purse that was left there and shoved the money and credit cards into his shirt. Well, we ran up to the lifeguard, who contacted the local police, and they arrested the guy.

After that, my daughter wouldn't let me out of her sight for the rest of the day. She stuck to me like glue. She said, "Mom, I'm scared. That was my very first bad guy." Well, I had to agree with her judgment that, based on his behavior, he was definitely a bad guy.

When Jesus tells us "do not judge," he does not relieve us of the need for discerning right from wrong. Rather, he condemns unjust and hypocritical judging of others. Christ gave us his perfect example of a nonjudgmental and forgiving attitude when he said to the crowd who was ready to stone the woman caught in adultery, "If any one of you is without sin, let him be the first to throw a stone at her" (John 8:7). What joy and peace we experience knowing that Christ no longer holds our sins against us, but has forgiven us through his sacrifice on the cross once and for all! And what joy and peace we experience when we also pardon and forgive our neighbors just as Christ has done for us!

Prayer: Dear Father, I praise and thank you for the sacrifice of your Son. Give me an attitude adjustment, Lord, and help me to …

Building Others Up

Invocation: In the name of the Father and of the Son and of the Holy Spirit. Amen.

Text: Do not let any unwholesome talk come out of your mouths, but only what is helpful for building others up according to their needs, that it may benefit those who listen. Eph. 4:29

Insight: "If you can't say something nice, then don't say anything at all." How many times as a child I heard that from my mother! And how many times I've said the same words to my children! Still, I know that this is not everything that God calls us to do in the Eighth Commandment.

Not lying and not speaking any other "unwholesome talk" about my neighbor might be a legalistic minimum, but God went far beyond that for me—and for you. Because God has chosen to love you, the crown of his creation, and to love you so much that he sent his Son to die for you, I can only assume that you are worth praising, defending, and speaking well of. Because God does that for both of us, I want to do so, too.

None of us is worthy of this treatment. We are all sinners. Yet isn't that just like God—the God we know because of Christ? He loves us. What a privilege we have to allow our neighbors a glimpse of Jesus through how we, as neighbors, talk with them and speak of them to others!

Prayer: Dear Jesus, forgive me for the unkind things I have said in the past. Help me to see my neighbors as you see them. Help me to speak the best of my neighbors, especially …

Holding My Tongue

Invocation: In the name of the Father and of the Son and of the Holy Spirit. Amen.

Text: A man who lacks judgment derides his neighbor, but a man of understanding holds his tongue. Prov. 11:12

Insight: Have you ever walked away from a confrontational discussion with someone and, after mulling it over in your mind, wished you had said something else—or hadn't said what you said? The text may encourage us to hold our tongue, but in today's world of aggressive business, hectic lifestyles, inconsiderate actions, long lines of people wherever you go, traffic jams, and who knows what all else, exercising self-control is not always easy. In fact, on the level of international politics, Roosevelt's speak-softly-and-carry-a-big-stick policy—the exact opposite of not deriding a neighbor and holding one's tongue—added to the verbal posturing against the former USSR and is the reason some claim that the West won the Cold War.

Ah, yes (we are told), timidity will get you the short end of the stick every time. At least so it seems.

The King James Version of today's Bible verse uses the word *wisdom* for "lacks judgment." If *you* were to list five words that describe the person who lives according to this text, would you have included the word *wise?* Maybe; maybe not. The problem is in choosing the context for defining the term *wisdom.* Consider these excerpts from St. Paul:

Has not God made foolish the wisdom of the world? … God was pleased through the foolishness of what was preached to save those who believe. … Christ [is] the power of God and the wisdom of God. For the foolishness of God is wiser than man's wisdom, and the weakness of God is stronger than man's strength. …

God chose the foolish things of the world to shame the wise … so that no one may boast before him. It is because of him that you are in Christ Jesus, who has become for us wisdom from God—that is, our righteousness, holiness and redemption. Therefore, as it is written: "Let him who boasts boast in the Lord."

When I came to you, brothers, … I resolved to know nothing while I was with you except Jesus Christ and him crucified. … My message and my preaching were not with wise and persuasive words, but with a demonstration of the Spirit's power, so that your faith might not rest on men's wisdom, but on God's power.

We do, however, speak a message of wisdom among the mature, but not the wisdom of this age or of the rulers of this age, who are coming to nothing. No, we speak of God's secret wisdom, a wisdom that has been hidden and that God destined for our glory before time began (1 Cor. 1:20, 21, 24–25, 27, 29–31; 2:2, 4–7).

So—what is wise, what is wisdom? Although rough language to and about others may gain us a temporary advantage, "what good is it for a man to gain the whole world, yet forfeit his soul?" (Mark 8:36). Not only that, but peace between people (as well as between countries) that is built on threats is no peace at all; it's only a temporary lull between wars.

God offers the only true wisdom: peace between humans built on the peace between God and people, which God alone creates through his Son. Christ was held up to ridicule, physical abuse, and humiliation during his suffering and death on the cross for us. He held his tongue and forgave his accusers—so that we might be forgiven for even the slips of our tongues and be made into the children of God.

True and lasting peace, both with God and with fellow human beings, grows out of forgiveness. You cannot be at peace with me as long as you savor my sins in your heart. And I cannot be at peace with you as long as I hold your sins against you. Jesus asks us instead—and enables us!—to look at each other the way he looks at us: as forgiven by him.

Now, that is wisdom. Peace to you. Amen.

Prayer: Dear Heavenly Father, help me to control my thoughts, words and actions. Especially give me strength when …

WORSHIP IDEAS

Hymn Suggestions

"Jesus! Name of Wondrous Love"

"Oh, for a Thousand Tongues to Sing"

"We Are One in the Bond of Love"

"We Will Glorify"

"Lord, Take My Hand and Lead Me"

"The Gift of Love"

Opening Sentences

Pastor: In the holy and powerful name of our God: Father, Son, and Holy Spirit.

People: Amen.

Pastor: Friends in Christ: In calling you "Christians," God has given you a good name, that of his Son. You bear with it the reputation of the Lord. It is an honor and a responsibility. You are to protect your new name, not only as you bear it yourself, but as you help your brother or sister bear it as well. Today we give ourselves to the Word of God that enbles us to protect the name of our neighbor, especially those who are of the household of faith, as we protect our own name—for both have been given by the Lord.

People: God help us to do so.

Pastor: Let us praise the name of our Lord and our God.

Confession of Sin

Pastor: We confess our sins and failures to God, our dear Father.

All: Father, today we confess the sins of the tongue. With it we praise you, our Lord and Father, and with it we curse people, who have been made in your likeness. Forgive us for Jesus' sake, cleanse our lips with the coals of your love and mercy, and purge our tongues so that they may speak well of our neighbors, explaining all their actions in the best possible way. Amen.

Absolution

Pastor: God has touched your heart with his love. He has washed it in the cleansing blood of his Son and has given you a new heart through the waters of Baptism. Empowered with his Spirit he now gives you words that are formed by your tongue and flow from your lips to bless and not curse, to praise and not defame.

People: Amen.

Scripture Readings

Lector: Each of you must put off falsehood and speak truthfully to his neighbor, for we are all members of one body (Eph. 4:25).

People: A gossip betrays a confidence, but a trustworthy man keeps a secret (Prov. 11:13).

Lector: If your brother sins against you, go and show him his fault, just between the two of you (Matt. 18:15).

People: Brothers, do not slander one another (James 4:11).

Lector: Speak up for those who cannot speak for themselves, for the rights of all who are destitute. Speak up and judge fairly; defend the rights of the poor and needy (Prov. 31:8).

People: [Love] always protects, always trusts, always hopes, always perseveres (1 Cor. 13:7).

Lector: Love covers over a multitude of sins (1 Peter 4:8).

TABLE CARD INSTRUCTIONS

How to use the table card:

1. Fold the card along the dotted lines to form a triangle. Staple, glue, or tape together.

2. Display for an effective reminder of this week's commandment and Scripture reference.

FOLD

Your reputation is safe with me.

Eighth Commandment

You shall not give false testimony against your neighbor.

FOLD

Speak up for those who cannot speak for themselves, for the rights of all who are destitute. Speak up and judge fairly; defend the rights of the poor and needy.

Prov. 31:8–9

FOLD

THE NINTH AND TENTH COMMANDMENTS

SERMON

Grace, mercy, and peace from God our Father and from our Lord and Savior, Jesus Christ.

Today we look at the Ninth and Tenth Commandments: Don't covet. To *covet,* basically means "to desire," "to take pleasure in." Here, of course, the idea is that we should not get hyper over whatever our neighbor has that we don't have. Don't take such pleasure in those things your neighbor has that your desiring becomes lust.

How serious is the problem, though? I don't know—how many of us are guilty of coveting? May I see a show of hands?

[NOTE: If necessary, ask again for a show of hands. Everyone could raise their hands, but some people fear sticking out in a crowd and won't raise their hands for anything. That's okay. Since the sin under discussion is "only" coveting, enough listeners will respond to enable the next point to be made.]

Interesting! The fact that some people were willing to raise their hands and that others of you were just about to do the same says something about how serious we think the sin of coveting is—or is not. If I had asked for all the adulterers to raise their hands, how many would have done so? And how many murderers? Yet as we studied these commandments, we know we are guilty of these too.

So, what's the problem? The problem is that we think coveting is no big thing. But adultery? Very few people will raise their hand for that one!

We don't worry very often about people who break the Ninth or Tenth Commandments—or even if we ourselves do. After all, stealing, adultery, murder, ruining people—those sins actually hurt people. And if I were to be caught committing such sins openly, I myself could suffer great consequences. But coveting?

And what is it we're not supposed to lust after? "You shall not covet your neighbor's house. You shall not covet your neighbor's wife, or his manservant or maidservant, his ox or donkey, or anything that belongs to your neighbor."

I know; it's been a long time since you've lusted after somebody else's manservant and/or ox. Besides, coveting is the American way. We even say,

"He who dies with the most toys wins." "Grab all you can get." As a matter of fact, capitalism is based on coveting. Our heroes are those who accrue the most wealth. And although we'll never have that amount of money, at least we can continue to buy whatever advertising says we want, just so we can pamper our own egos. Where would advertising and TV commercials be if they couldn't count on our ability to covet? Our society likes coveting; even our movies are based on it. Do what you want, when you want; that's the motto of the movies. And we love it!

People have always had a craving, a desire for physical things. What's the latest fad toy? It doesn't matter *what* it is, we want it. It used to be GI Joe. Some here today may remember when they just *had* to mail in those box tops for the Lone Ranger Secret Decoder Ring. And what about the adult toys that have now become necessities—computer note pads, personal-use cellular phones, motorboats and second homes, whatever. And before that—how long ago?—the 1950s family's first TV. And before that, player pianos. And before that, a surrey with a fringe on top. And before that, two Sunday outfits instead of just one. And before that, … Well, how far back should we go? What comes before coveting your neighbor's manservant and/or ox?

Sad to say, and this has always been true, we humans covet so much so strongly that *things* become more important to us than people. People used to shake their heads in disbelief when the old cowboy movies claimed that stealing a man's horse was punishable by death. But then a year or two ago, a segment on TV's *20/20* showed a man shooting a car thief in the back—even though the theft was botched up and the owner had not in fact lost his car.

Reality for too many is that things are more important than people, and they're more important than relationships. Our two-job families barely have enough time for each other and the children. Relationships, though, need time, not stuff.

"You shall not covet."

Why? Why should we not do this? God doesn't explain in Exodus 20, but he does elsewhere—a number of times. We should not covet because that sin is a root cause behind all the sins against the second table of the Law. I covet the right to do as I please, so I reject authority. If you stand in the way of my getting what I want, I have the right to kill you. If I want your husband or wife, it's my right to do what I please. If you don't know how to protect your stuff, finders keepers. And don't challenge me, or I'll spread all over town what I know about *you*. So don't get in my way when I want to indulge in a little bit of harmless coveting. Get me?

We need to hear what God says about coveting, about the desires of our hearts going wacko.

In James 4:1–2 (NKJV) he says,

> Where do wars and fights come from among you? Do they not come from your desires for pleasure that war in your members? You lust and do not

have. You murder and covet and can not obtain. You fight and war.

War—now there's something serious. Very serious! Especially if we have a child or somebody close to the family who is on foreign soil or getting ready to go there right now. When that happens to our family, we become very concerned. War is serious; people die. Yet, where do these wars and fights come from? They begin with coveting.

I am not suggesting that every act of coveting concludes with war between two countries—or even between two people. However, when we treat covetousness as less serious than it is, we allow it to grow in our own hearts as well as in the hearts of those around us.

Is coveting a serious sin? It is even worse than we would first imagine. In the Old Testament, Job tells us a very revealing thing: "If I have put my trust in gold, … then these also would be sins to be judged, for I would have been unfaithful to God on high" (Job 31:24, 28).

Ah, yes; gold—a nice house, more money, the lottery. None of you have gotten upset when you didn't win the lottery, have you? No, I didn't think so! Job said that trusting things would be equal to denying God. If I put my trust in gold, put my trust in winning that lottery, this would be a sin to be judged, for I would have been unfaithful to God.

Coveting is *not* such a small thing. It is an idolatry that replaces God and encourages us to treat other people as less than human, as less than the special creations of God that they are.

Listen as I read again in James:

> Each one is tempted when, by his own evil desire, he is dragged away and enticed. Then, after desire has conceived, it gives birth to sin; and sin, when it is full-grown, gives birth to death. Don't be deceived, my dear brothers (1:14–16).

Death is a serious thing. That's where coveting leads.

Like you, I am a child of the American way. Covetousness has run rampant in my life many times. And it would be much easier for me to preach a sermon that said, "Oh, well. I don't have an answer; I'm a coveter just like you. Let's go on coveting."

Praise God, I'm not up here to preach my own ideas, but his. And he does have some ideas about how we are to war against this sin. God points to it in his words to the young preacher Timothy, but the counsel applies to us all:

> Godliness with contentment is great gain. For we brought nothing into the world, and we can take nothing out of it. But if we have food and clothing, we will be content with that. People who want to get rich fall into temptation and a trap and into many foolish and harmful desires that plunge men into ruin and destruction. For the love of money is a root of all kinds of evil. Some people, eager for money, have wandered from the faith and pierced themselves with many griefs.

But you, O man of God [Timothy], flee from all this, and pursue righteousness, godliness, faith, love, endurance and gentleness (1 Tim. 6:6–11).

There is the answer. How do you deal with coveting? You flee it. The problem is, that's like trying to pick yourself up by your own bootstraps.

Scripture offers three helps on the process of dealing with covetousness.

The first step is to realize what God's Word says about coveting: namely, that true evil is not just our outward actions but also our inner thoughts. Matthew 15 tells us,

> The things that come out of the mouth come from the heart, and these make a man "unclean." For out of the heart come evil thoughts, murder, adultery, sexual immorality, theft, false testimony, slander (vv. 18–19).

We think that the evil we can hide in our heart is no evil at all. But as God points out in his Word, inner coveting *is* evil—by itself—and it leads to outward evil as well.

So, the first step in fleeing covetousness is to hear what God says about us and this sin: that we are not righteous or great. If you are a visitor here today, I welcome you to a congregation of sinners—but sinners who seek God's forgiveness.

And that leads us to the second step: That we confess our sins.

The psalmist says, "All my longings lie open before you, O Lord" (Ps. 38:9). God knows everything. We cannot hide our sins from him. We cannot act as if we are somebody different from what we are. God knows our hearts. And so we might as well just open up and confess and say, "Lord, this is what I'm like, but I know I need to change. Yet I also know I cannot change by myself."

That leads to the third step: to rely on God for his mercy and grace. We need his mercy, his forgiveness, for without it we are yet in our sin and will not change. Therefore I announce to you who confess your covetousness and are contrite before God: God does forgive you because of Jesus, your Savior. He was punished for your sin, and he died so that you might live.

Having received the mercy of God, we also receive the grace of God. Although we often use the terms *mercy* and *grace* interchangeably, they are not the same. *Mercy* refers to **not** receiving what we deserve (punishment), and *grace* refers to receiving what we do not deserve—all God's good gifts.

The first and the best gift he has ever and could ever give to us is faith—faith that Jesus did die for us, faith that because of him we are the forgiven children of God, faith that we are living in the kingdom of God and will continue to do so throughout eternity.

> Do not worry, saying, "What shall we eat?" or "What shall we drink?" or "What shall we wear?" For the pagans run after all these things, and your heavenly Father knows that you need them. But seek first his kingdom and his righteousness, and all these things will be given to you as well. Therefore do not worry about tomorrow, for tomorrow will worry about itself. Each day has enough trouble of its own (Matt. 6:31–34).

If you missed the point, Jesus repeats himself, "If you, then, though you are evil, know how to give good gifts to your children, how much more will your Father in heaven give good gifts to those who ask him!" (Matt. 7:11).

God knows our need much better than we ever could. He knows exactly what we need to have a joyous life. God is saying, "You don't need to covet after things; you don't have to think about how you are going to get these things. I *want* to bless you." Listen to these words from Ps. 37:4–5. Although David spoke them about God in the third person, I'm going to paraphrase them as if God were speaking them in the first person:

> Delight yourself in me, and I will give you the desires of your heart. Commit your way to me; trust in me and I will do this.

"Covet?" the pure in heart ask. "Why? God has given me everything I need—first for eternity and then for the support and wants of this body. There is nothing left to covet."

A member of one congregation could not pay her rent. She told the pastor the truth: "I have no money, and I have nothing to sell anymore, for I have sold almost everything I own. Now I cannot pay my rent, and they're going to kick me out. I'm going to be homeless. If there is a way the church can help me, I'd really appreciate it."

The church did help—and by happenstance, the next Sunday the sermon was on the way God provides for his people. After the service, the woman told her pastor, "You know, I don't think I really understood the gift that I received from the church, because I was so busy thinking I had received it from the church. I now realize that God provided that gift and that God will provide all that I need. Thank you for helping me to put the gifts of God that I have in perspective. I don't know where next month's rent is going to come from, but I do know that God is in charge. Thank you."

What a lesson she had learned: God likes to give; that's his very nature! Before we ever ask he has said already, "I do want to bless you; here, I'll find a way."

Christians used to say one prayer so often that a number of restaurants set a printed version on their tables. It's from Ps. 145:15–16 (KJV). I'm going to read a few more verses in addition.

> The eyes of all wait upon thee; and thou givest them their meat in due season.
>
> Thou openest thine hand, and satisfiest the desire of every living thing.
>
> The LORD is righteous in all his ways, and holy in all his works.
>
> The LORD is nigh unto all them that call upon him, to all that call upon him in truth.
>
> He will fulfil the desire of them that fear him.

There, in the Lord, is the answer to coveting and the Ninth and Tenth Commandments. May our Lord so bless you. Amen.

Life Is More than Possessions

Invocation: In the name of the Father and of the Son and of the Holy Spirit. Amen.

Text: Watch out! Be on your guard against all kinds of greed; a man's life does not consist in the abundance of his possessions. Luke 12:15

Insight: Have you ever seen the bumper sticker, "Whoever dies with the most toys, wins"? It's easy to retort, "How foolish!" However, do our actions speak a different reality? Are we building earthly treasures, caring little about building Christ's kingdom on earth?

A friend of mine was feeling very lucky. His son had been accepted to the college of his choice in spite of huge odds against him. Then my friend sold his house on the very last day of his agreement with his Realtor. If it had not sold, he would have lost out on a contingency offer he had on another house, a single-story house he needed because of his wife's poor health. He was feeling so lucky, he called his wife and told her, "Trust me; buy some lottery tickets."

It's easy to be greedy, to want more. "After all," some would say, "it's only human." Yes, it is human—sinfully so. That's why Christ warns us, "Watch out!" and points us to the parable of the rich man who built barn after barn, only to die without God.

The Good News? Because of Christ, we do not have to worry about possessions. We belong to God, and he promises to take care of all our needs. And what about our toys? Why— share them, of course. That way we don't have to own them all.

Prayer: Lord of all, provider of all our needs, come into my heart, help control my human desires for more riches. Let me understand that …

Delighting in the Lord

Invocation: In the name of the Father and of the Son and of the Holy Spirit. Amen.

Text: Delight yourself in the LORD and he will give you the desires of your heart. Ps. 37:4

Insight: Our text offers up a challenge of sorts. We are challenged to do good, to trust God and not to worry—all of this in the midst of our wicked world. In fact, we are to do more than that; we are to "delight," that is, take great pleasure in the Lord.

"Delight yourself." Sounds like a call to action. Sounds like simply committing one hour per week to church and worship might only be a good beginning. Sounds like a call to study his Word, to live a life in him, and to share his redemption with others as well.

The beautiful truth is that through the Holy Spirit we are given hearts that do delight in him. We actually can delight in his love, in his will for us, and in his Word. It's his work in us as we focus on Jesus rather than on cars and pizza and all the rest of the stuff that TV says we should have.

When God works his will in us, we are led to a life of worship. Therefore we can sing with King David, "I rejoiced with those who said to me, 'Let us go to the house of the LORD.'" (Ps. 122:1).

Prayer: Lord, help us to be bold with our faith and trust in you, to take great pleasure in you. Stand beside us as we study your Word and seek purity of heart and your will. Protect us from those things that would lead us astray. Be with us today as we …

Contentment Is True Gain

Invocation: In the name of the Father and of the Son and of the Holy Spirit. Amen.

Text: Godliness with contentment is great gain. 1 Tim. 6:6

Insight: Webster defines *contentment* as being satisfied—and for the most part, we are. Make a list sometime of the hundreds of times a day when you're satisfied: A good cup of coffee in the morning, a job, a family, plenty to eat, health. God wants those things for us, but there's more to contentment than "things." Life isn't always smooth. Sometimes it's easier to be dissatisfied.

I spent about a year out of work. A lot happens to a person who has had a successful working life and then, rather abruptly, finds him- or herself unemployed. Lots of doubts creep in. My faith was sorely tested when I asked, "If God wants me to be satisfied, why am I unemployed?" What I learned is that God wants me to be content even when I am unemployed.

What God wants is for each of us to be content *in him*. He sent his only Son to die for our sins. He has redeemed us. We can be strong in the knowledge that he is our salvation. Not a job. Not our health. Not our bank account. The "great gain" of 1 Tim. 6:6 is to be satisfied, content through Christ's presence in our lives.

Prayer: Dear Lord, as we remember that you are our only true source of contentment, we pray that you would help us today, especially as we …

Satisfied with God

Invocation: In the name of the Father and of the Son and of the Holy Spirit. Amen.

Text: Keep your lives free from the love of money and be content with what you have, because God has said, "Never will I leave you; never will I forsake you." Heb. 13:5

Insight: How well we know that the love of money is the root of all evil! Some people, eager for money, have wandered from the faith. And, faith is the real issue—the only issue.

Have you ever felt alone, afraid, unsure, scared? Have you been part of a family breakup or known someone struggling with life's difficulties? We're told with staggering statistics that each of us will be the victim of some sort of crime in our lifetime. Economic chaos has left many people uncertain of future security. It's easy to understand why people sometimes feel like they have been abandoned by God himself and therefore wander from their faith and…

Hold everything! God has made a covenant with us, a promise: "Never will I leave you; never will I forsake you." Jesus, the Great Shepherd, gives us love, forgiveness, mercy, and all the other gifts in our spiritual life. He gives us hope, because he died and rose and lives with us now.

Money? It may be a necessary evil, but Jesus is the one fortune that will never fail us.

Prayer: Dear Father, you who sealed your covenant with us, lift us when we fall. Don't let money, possessions, or bad times cloud our faith. Strengthen our love for you and our trust in your promise, especially when …

WORSHIP IDEAS

Hymn Suggestions

"All Depends on Our Possessing"

"Take My Life, O Lord, Renew"

"Here Is the Tenfold Sure Command"

"We Are One in the Bond of Love "

"How Majestic Is Your Name"

Confession of Sins

All: It is hard to hear this word, Heavenly Father. We want to think that we are basically upright in heart. But your Word cuts to the quick and reveals that our hearts lust after what is not ours. We do covet what you have given to others. We repent and seek your mercy once again. We know that you are merciful and long-suffering. Look not upon our sins, but look upon the atoning blood of your Son. Create in us a new heart, and put your willing Spirit within us.

Absolution

Pastor: Hear the word of the Lord: "I will give you a new heart and put a new spirit in you; I will remove from you your heart of stone and give you a heart of flesh. And I will put my Spirit in you and move you to follow my decrees and be careful to keep my laws ... You will be my people, and I will be your God" (Ezek. 36:26–28).

People: Amen.

Scripture Readings

Lector: Out of the heart come evil thoughts, murder, adultery, sexual immorality, theft, false testimony, slander (Matt. 15:19).

People: Woe to those who plan iniquity ... They covet fields and seize them, and houses, and take them. They defraud a man of his home, a fellowman of his inheritance (Micah 2:1, 2).

Lector: If we have food and clothing, we will be content with that. People who want to get rich fall into temptation and a trap and into many foolish and harmful desires that plunge men into ruin and destruction. For the love of money is a root of all kinds of evil. Some people, eager for money, have wandered from the faith and pierced themselves with many griefs (1 Tim. 6:8–10).

People: Watch out! Be on your guard against all kinds of greed; a man's life does not consist in the abundance of his possessions (Luke 12:15).

Lector: Godliness with contentment is great gain (1 Tim. 6:6).

People: Delight yourself in the LORD and he will give you the desires of your heart (Ps. 37:4).

TABLE CARD INSTRUCTIONS

How to use the table card:

1. Fold the card along the dotted lines to form a triangle. Staple, glue, or tape together.
2. Display for an effective reminder of this week's commandment and Scripture reference.

.... FOLD

Godliness with contentment is great gain.

Ninth Commandment
You shall not covet your neighbor's house.

Tenth Commandment
You shall not covet your neighbor's wife, or his manservant or maidservant, his ox or donkey, or anything that belongs to your neighbor.

.... FOLD

Be content with what you have, because God has said,

"Never will I leave you; never will I forsake you."

Heb. 13:5

.... FOLD

The Close of the Commandments

SERMON

Grace be unto you, mercy, and peace in the name of the triune God, the Father, the Son, and the Spirit. Amen.

How often we sing our praises to God for his loving care for the world! The words of King David are our words:

> Sing to [the LORD] a new song; play skillfully, and shout for joy. … The LORD loves righteousness and justice; the earth is full of his unfailing love (Ps. 33:3, 5).

Listen, though, to one pastor's [the author's] story of peace and love. He was part of a tour group to Palestine in 1995. He writes:

> It was in Bethlehem that we experienced something very powerful, a frightful tension between evil and good, between wrath and infinite love.

> Bethlehem is an Arabic city, but we were coming into it inside an Israeli bus with an Israeli driver and an Israeli guide. We could feel the tension and the nervousness as we rode into the city where Jesus was born. When we came to the site, the guide and the driver said, "Now; we park here! You walk right straight over there into the Shrine of the Nativity—the Church of the Nativity. Don't go off into the streets; just go there." We obeyed, for fear of our lives.

> Back on the bus, we went to a place where we could get some wood carvings. Again, when we got to the parking spot, we got out of the bus and went directly into the building.

> We could feel the tension of how easily a peace could be broken open and spill out bloodshed.

> But then we went someplace else: to the garden tomb, outside the walls of Jerusalem. There in a garden we visited a first-century tomb hewn out of solid rock, complete with the ridges where you could roll a stone in front of the door.

> Now, we do not know and never will, whether that's the exact tomb in which Jesus was buried. We do know it was from the first century and that only one body had lain in it. Maybe it was Jesus' tomb.

> But what was profound was that *there* was a place of peace and love. It was the highlight of the trip for almost every one of us.

Problem: How do we reconcile the truth of God's rule of love—and true it is, because God says it of himself—with another truth we see in the world: people destroying and ruining one another?

I am amazed when joy can be halted so quickly by the terror of the world. Consider, for example, the fantastic celebration of the peace accord signing in the Mideast that was destroyed by the murder of Yitzhak Rabin. Consider how many people were involved in mini celebrations in life when their world came to an end in the Oklahoma City bombing or the bombing of the World Trade Center. Consider a mother boasting about her child's first kindergarten paper when a drive-by shooting takes the child.

The horror! The confusion! Yes, God rules with love—but where is his rod against the horror in the world? How do love and justice fit together?

The answer lies in one word in our text for today: the word *jealous*. We read from Ex. 20:5–6:

> I, the LORD your God, am a jealous God, punishing the children for the sin of the fathers to the third and fourth generation of those who hate me, but showing love to a thousand generations of those who love me and keep my commandments.

The word *jealous,* of course, does not mean that God is like a jealous lover who cannot stand to see his girlfriend talk to anyone else for fear that he's going to lose her. Hardly. That kind of jealousy is not rooted in love but in a profound insecurity about one's self. It is the belief that one is not worthy to be loved. God is not so insecure. Nor is he controlled by emotions.

Therefore, when God calls himself "a jealous God," he is talking about something else. The dictionary helps us a little bit. It defines *jealousy* as "vigilant in guarding a possession."

Ah, yes. Now it makes sense. God has made us as his possession, and he is vigilant in guarding us. Why? We know that the reason is his infinite love. Like a father, he is jealous for his family and therefore is not going to let harm and danger come to it.

That's the picture of our jealous God: He vigilantly guards us, his possession, because he has given to us himself as our God.

The connection between God's creative love and his jealousy is made obvious by the place where God speaks of his jealousy. It does not come at the end of the listing of the Ten Commandments in Exodus, but right after the First Commandment and its explanation (Ex. 20:3–6).

> You shall have no other gods before me. You shall not make for yourself an idol in the form of anything in heaven above or on the earth beneath or in the waters below. You shall not bow down to them or worship them; …

And now comes the text:

> For I, the LORD your God, am a jealous God, punishing the children for the sin of the fathers to the third and fourth generation of those who hate me, but showing love to a thousand generations of those who love me and keep my commandments.

We call these words "the close" of the commandments because they form a type of *closure* to them. The words emphasize that all the commandments, from first to last, stand or fall on the fact that the God of Scripture, *Yahweh,* is the only God and is *our* God. God is saying, I gave myself to you to be your God. I am the one who called you out of Egypt (Ex. 20:1). Long before that I promised to your fathers, to Abraham, Isaac, and Jacob, that I would be your God. I am the one who has continued that promise through my only-begotten Son, Jesus Christ. You, the ones grafted into the family of Abraham (Rom. 11:17–21): I brought you out of slavery to sin to the freedom of my love. *Therefore,*

You shall have no other gods before me.

Then, having reminded us of his loving jealousy *for our good,* he goes on to give the rest of the commandments. They flow like a chain, bound together at the clasp of the First Commandment along with the closure: I am your God. Don't run to another, for I jealously love and guard you.

Well, some ask, if he is vigilant in guarding his possessions, *how* does he guard us? The answer is clear. He guards us by giving us these commandments, which are, first of all, a working relationship with himself and then with all other people.

Every commandment deals with his guarding us, his possessions. Through the commandments God is saying in effect,

Use my name to bless each other. In my name, take a day of rest to worship me. Because I take care of you both directly and through representatives, give my representatives—parents and all in authority—the respect and obedience you give me. And, because I take care of each of you through each of you, don't kill or even hurt one another. Instead, participate with me in creating new life, a new generation, through marital sex (and I stress marital sex because without marriage, you'll revert to hurting one another). And further, protect what I give to everyone else, because when everyone protects everyone else's stuff, then you don't have to worry about your own. Protect their possessions as well as their reputation. In fact, don't even covet what is your neighbor's. I have told these things to your neighbors so that through them I might protect you; and I tell these things to you so that through you I might protect them.

In summary, God gives to us those Ten Commandments as a means of a working, loving relationship through which we can experience blessings from him.

But God also guards us in another way: He shows to us how serious he is about his laws by warning us of his wrath.

I, the LORD your God, am a jealous God, punishing the children for the sin of the fathers to the third and fourth generation of those who hate me (Ex. 20:5).

Now, the moment that we hear wrath, our natural tendency is to think of fire and brimstone—especially when we want it rained down upon someone who has harmed us. But do you know the way the wrath of God is revealed primarily?

Turn with me to Rom. 1:18.

The wrath of God is being revealed from heaven against all the godlessness and wickedness of men who suppress the truth by their wickedness.

And then in verses 24, 26, and 28 God tells us *how* that wrath will be revealed:

> God gave them over in the sinful desires of their hearts to sexual impurity for the degrading of their bodies with one another. ... God gave them over to shameful lusts. ... Since they did not think it worthwhile to retain the knowledge of God, he gave them over to a depraved mind, to do what ought not to be done.

Do you see what the wrath of God is? The wrath of God ultimately is turning people over to their own sinful passions.

Do you know what happens when the passions of humans run unchecked? Think of the international news of the last few years. Look at Rwanda, the passion of hate by tribe against tribe. Look at Bosnia, Serbia, Croatia, the hatred by ethnic groups against each other. Look at Haiti, the passion of greed in some running the government at the expense of all the populace.

[Here the preacher will want to keep the examples current by citing contemporary international, national, and local examples.]

And what would happen if you allowed the passion of hate that you sometimes feel to go unchecked in your life? What would happen if you allowed the lust that you feel in your heart from time to time go unchecked? What would happen if you allowed your tongue to say whatever it feels like saying and never be checked by God? What would it do?

You see? That's the passions of humans run amok. God gave his commandments to check that kind of stuff, so that the wrath of God is not experienced, so that he does not turn us over to our own passions.

But it's right there, brothers and sisters, where we find ourself needing to fall on our knees again before God. Like it or not, we have all given ourselves over to our passions time and again. We have honored other gods, thereby misusing the name of *Yahweh*. We have dishonored his representatives; we have mentally and sometimes physically abused other peoples' bodies and possessions. And God alone knows how much we have coveted after the things of this world. It is to *you*, to *me*, that God threatens punishment to the third and fourth generations—punishment to our grandchildren and great-grandchildren for the sins we have committed.

"How?" we cry. "How can we ever get the blessing of God to a thousand generations of those who love him and keep his commandments?"

The answer is always in our Lord Jesus Christ. For you see, the good news is that God in his infinite love—a love greater than his wrath—saw fit to send for us a substitute to keep that Law perfectly. And the punishment we deserve for our sin God laid upon the shoulders of his Son. And what did Jesus do with them? He went to the cross. And what happened there? The wrath of God revealed against sin was poured out upon Jesus. And the ultimate wrath—the tearing of one apart from God, the abandonment of God—

was experienced by Jesus, and he cried out, "My God, my God, why have you forsaken me?" (Matt. 27:46).

Let's go back to the frustration expressed at the beginning of the sermon. I asked, "How do we reconcile the truth of God's rule of love with another truth we see in the world: people destroying and ruining one another?" I called attention to the murder of Yitzhak Rabin and the bombings in Oklahoma City and the World Trade Center.

How do God's love and his wrath, his justice, fit together? They came together on Calvary. There his jealousy on our behalf played itself before the whole world. Now, therefore, the commandments no longer terrorize us but guide us in responding to such a loving God, who revealed himself in Jesus Christ and led us out of slavery to sin.

Talk about love! What love, that God should so love us! How can we not love him in return? And that, my dear friends, is the living of the commandments.

In Matt. 22:34–40, just three or four days before the crucifixion, the Pharisees persuaded an expert of the Law to try to trick Jesus concerning the Law. At that point no one realized the strict obedience to the Law that Jesus would perform on Calvary. Instead, the expert asked about forcing others to obey the Law. "Teacher," he asked, "which is the greatest commandment in the Law?" Jesus replied:

> "Love the Lord your God with all your heart and with all your soul and with all your mind." This is the first and greatest commandment. And the second is like it: "Love your neighbor as yourself." All the Law and the Prophets hang on these two commandments.

Recall again that pastor's visit to the Holy Land and his experience of peace there. That's the way it should be. For it is at the resurrection of our Lord where we see the jealousy of God being completed. He vigilantly guarded his possessions all the way into the death of his Son.

However, the Father also raised up Jesus in order that you and I could know that the wrath of God will not be placed upon us. Rather, we receive his blessing to a thousand generations. What love!

There! God, vigilant to guard his possession, gives to us his law for our relationship with him as well as with others. And when you love him with all your heart, with all your soul, and with all your mind, you will love your neighbor as yourself.

Now we begin to say to God, I do love you with my heart and soul—not by my own strength but by that strength that you give me in the Holy Spirit. And I will serve and love my neighbor. Not on my own power but out of that renewed and redeemed power that you give to me.

And thus we begin to live out our lives as Christian people, honoring and keeping his commandments and experiencing that blessing of God that speaks a blessing to the thousandth generation of those who love him and keep his commandments.

In the name of the Father and of the Son and of the Holy Spirit. Amen.

The Beginning of Wisdom

Invocation: In the name of the Father and of the Son and of the Holy Spirit. Amen.

Text: The fear of the LORD is the beginning of wisdom; all who follow his precepts have good understanding. To him belongs eternal praise. Ps. 111:10

Insight: Wisdom and old age seem to go together. But Scripture does not automatically relate the two. Instead, wisdom is related to God; he is the source and author of all wisdom.

What is God's wisdom? St. Paul answers,

We preach Christ crucified: a stumbling block to Jews and foolishness to Gentiles, but to those whom God has called, both Jews and Greeks, Christ the power of God and the wisdom of God (1 Cor. 1:23–24).

And in the "Scriptures, which are able to make you wise for salvation through faith in Christ Jesus" (2 Tim. 3:15), the Holy Spirit enlightens our minds to see that Jesus' life, death, and resurrection from the dead forgives our sins, gives us peace now, and hope for our future in heaven. That's wisdom!

Psalm 111:10 says that wisdom grows out of our relationship with God, out of our "fear," our faith. We believers want that wisdom to grow as we immerse ourselves in him and exercise our Christian "muscles" in our own lives, in our families, in our congregations, and in our secular community.

One evidence of wisdom is *prudence*—the search for balance and moderation in our lives. Prudence in God's wisdom seeks to live according to his will, the Ten Commandments, under the Holy Spirit's guidance and inspiration.

An ancient prayer of the church expresses this well:

Prayer: Almighty and everlasting God, give us such a measure of your mercy, that we, running the way of your commandments, may receive your heavenly promises made sure to us through the suffering and death of Jesus Christ, in whose name we pray. Amen.

Fear of the Lord

Invocation: In the name of the Father and of the Son and of the Holy Spirit. Amen.

Text: The fear of the LORD is the beginning of wisdom; all who follow his precepts have good understanding. To him belongs eternal praise. Ps. 111:10

Insight: *Fear* seems to be a strange word to describe our relationship with God. At Halloween we fear ghosts, goblins, and things that go bump in the night. Sometimes we fear being honest with ourselves or with our friends, because we are afraid of what they might say. This type of fear also occurs in the Bible. When Adam and Eve sinned, they tried to hide from God, because they were afraid of him.

Actually, fear deals more with the future than the present. We are fearful in the present because we do not know the future. We are afraid now when we are unsure what will happen to us. We are afraid when we believe that the future will be bad.

To help us overcome that fear, the psalmist proclaims, "The fear of the LORD is the beginning of wisdom." Here, though, the word *fear* means "awesome respect." And that we give God because of the Gospel, the Good News of Jesus Christ. In it we hear God's eternal "Do not be afraid!" We do not shrink back, because through Jesus Christ we know God loves us, forgives us, and keeps us as his very own. He protects and guards us even when there are "ghosts and goblins and things that go bump in the night."

This week take some time to write down your fears, your "ghosts and goblins." Describe how God through his love and power makes you strong and fearless.

Prayer: Almighty and everlasting God, you are always ready to give more than we desire or deserve. Pour out upon us an abundance of your mercy, forgiving us those things of which our conscience is afraid. In the name of your Son, we ask also that you give us ...

A Good Understanding

Invocation: In the name of the Father and of the Son and of the Holy Spirit. Amen.

Text: The fear of the LORD is the beginning of wisdom; all who follow his precepts have good understanding. To him belongs eternal praise. Ps. 111:10

Insight: Have you noticed the theme in this study on the Ten Commandments? God's commandments are to be our "to do" list. Since we are God's people through Baptism, God enables us to reflect our fear and love for him in our relationships with him and with each other. The psalms bring all of that together in one easy-to-remember verse: "The fear of the LORD is the beginning of wisdom; all who follow his precepts have good understanding."

Nurtured by God the Holy Spirit to "do" his commandments in our daily life and conversation, we begin to see that our priorities and purposes in life may differ from many of our associates, classmates, or acquaintances. For some people, winning is everything. Other people have to work at survival. As God's people, called to live according to his commandments, we choose to use God's principles whether we pursue success or survival. We pursue our goals under the umbrella of God's grace and will. That means we respect the person, relationships, property, and reputation of our neighbor.

That's not easy. God reminds us in the close of the commandments that our future, individually and collectively, is in his loving hands. Above everything else we trust in the divine mercy in Christ Jesus, which God showers upon all of us to a thousand generations.

Prayer: Grant us, Lord, your Spirit so we may think and do those things that are right so that we, enabled by your Spirit, may live according to your will. Especially we pray that …

To Him Belongs Eternal Praise

Invocation: In the name of the Father and of the Son and of the Holy Spirit. Amen.

Text: The fear of the LORD is the beginning of wisdom; all who follow his precepts have good understanding. To him belongs eternal praise. Ps. 111:10

Insight: Worship is acknowledging God's worth-ship and giving him what he deserves: our thanks and praise. The text starts out by reminding us that we who worship are those who fear the Lord, those who have a personal relationship with him. It is out of that relationship that our worship flows.

We worship God first because of who he is. Our living God intervenes in our history to create, redeem, and sanctify people who are his own: you and me.

We worship God second because of what he has done. God's Ten Commandments are a two-edged sword: they show our sin and, once we understand God's grace through Jesus the Savior, the commandments show us pathways to sanctification. Through the Gospel we know and believe that God himself in the person of Jesus Christ has forgiven our failings under the Law and has set our feet again firmly on the path of righteousness.

Through God's Word, we have learned and received what it means to live as God's people redeemed by grace. The prophet Micah outlines this for us:

[God] has showed you, O man, what is good. And what does the LORD require of you? To act justly and to love mercy and to walk humbly with your God (Micah 6:8).

Prayer: O God, the protector of all who trust in you, without whom nothing is strong, nothing holy, multiply upon us your mercy, so that with you as our Ruler and Guide we pass through things temporal and lose not things eternal; through Jesus Christ our Lord, in whose name we pray. Amen.

WORSHIP IDEAS

Hymn Suggestions

"How Great Thou Art"

"Evening and Morning"

"Have Thine Own Way, Lord"

"I Will Praise the Name"

Opening Sentences

Pastor: In the name of the Father and of the Son and of the Holy Spirit.

People: Amen.

Pastor: Hear the Word of the Lord for our worship today: "I, the LORD your God, am a jealous God, punishing the children for the sin of the fathers to the third and fourth generation of those who hate me, but showing love to a thousand generations of those who love me and keep my commandments" (Ex. 20:5–6).

People: This word is strong. Who can endure it?

Pastor: Yes, this word is strong, for our God is an awesome God. His wrath is to be feared, for he does not let the guilty off guiltless. But his love is stronger still. He is majestic in all he does to save us. Let us heed this word, then, even as we come to him in worship, both in fear and in trust.

Confession of Sins

Pastor: Have you kept all of these commandments in thought, word, and deed?

People: No, we have not. Therefore we fear the Lord's wrath.

Pastor: We need not be afraid of his wrath when we come to him in true sorrow for our sins and failures and seek his mercy for the sake of his Son, Jesus.

People: We come in sorrow and contrition. We confess our sins and seek his forgiveness.

All: O almighty God, merciful Father, I, a poor, miserable sinner, confess to you all my sins and iniquities with which I have ever offended you and justly deserved your punishment now and forever. But I am heartily sorry for them and sincerely repent of them, and I pray you of your boundless mercy and for the sake of the holy, innocent, bitter sufferings and death of your beloved Son, Jesus Christ, to be gracious and merciful to me, a poor sinful being. Amen.

Absolution

Pastor: Do you believe in Jesus Christ as your Savior from your sins?

People: Yes, I believe he died for me to remove the guilt of my sin.

Pastor: Then as you believe, so be it to you. I proclaim to you the forgiveness of all your sins, in the name of the Father, and of the Son, and of the Holy Spirit. God's wrath is now removed from before you. You can enter into his presence with praise and thanksgiving and experience anew his love.

People: Amen.

A Dialog on the Meaning of God as a Jealous God

Pastor: What does it mean that our awesome and majestic God is a jealous God? What does it mean that he will punish up to a fourth generation, and bless unto a thousand generations?

People: It means that we should fear God's wrath and not do anything against his commandments. But he promises grace and every blessing to all who keep these commandments. Therefore, trusting in the strength of his Son, we should also love and trust in God and gladly do what he commands.

Pastor: What are these commands?

People: They are ten. They are as follows:

- You shall have no other gods before me.
- You shall not misuse the name of the LORD your God.
- Remember the Sabbath day by keeping it holy.
- Honor your father and your mother, so that you may live long in the land the LORD your God is giving you.
- You shall not murder.
- You shall not commit adultery.
- You shall not steal.
- You shall not give false testimony against your neighbor.
- You shall not covet your neighbor's house.
- You shall not covet your neighbor's wife, or his manservant or maidservant, his ox or donkey, or anything that belongs to your neighbor.

TABLE CARD INSTRUCTIONS

How to use the table card:

1. Fold the card along the dotted lines to form a triangle. Staple, glue, or tape together.
2. Display for an effective reminder of this week's commandment and Scripture reference.

FOLD

Love fulfills the Law.

The Close of the Commandments

I, the LORD your God, am a jealous God, punishing the children for the sin of the fathers to the third and fourth generation of those who hate me, but showing love to a thousand generations of those who love me and keep my commandments.

FOLD

Do to others what you would have them do to you,

for this sums up the Law and the Prophets.

Matt. 7:12

FOLD